SELECTED
POEMS AND LETTERS OF
JOHN KEATS

THE POETRY BOOKSHELF

General Editor: James Reeves

SELECTED
POEMS AND LETTERS OF
JOHN KEATS

Edited with an Introduction and Commentary

by

ROBERT GITTINGS

HEINEMANN

Heinemann Educational Books Ltd

LONDON MELBOURNE TORONTO
SINGAPORE JOHANNESBURG
HONG KONG NAIROBI
AUCKLAND IBADAN

JOHN KEATS 1795–1821

INTRODUCTION AND COMMENTARY
© ROBERT GITTINGS 1966

SBN 435 15044 8 (cased edition)
SBN 435 15045 6 (paperback edition)

FIRST PUBLISHED 1966
REPRINTED 1968

Published by
Heinemann Educational Books Ltd
48 Charles Street, London W1X 8AH
Printed in Great Britain by Morrison and Gibb Ltd
London and Edinburgh

CONTENTS

FOREWORD

IN this selection of Keats's poems and letters, the poems are placed as nearly as possible in the order in which they were composed. The letters, or sections of letters, are interspersed with the poems, also in chronological order. Together they form a record of Keats's life and progress in poetry and in prose.

The text used for the poems is, with very few exceptions, that of H. W. Garrod, *The Poetical Works of John Keats*, 2nd edition, Clarendon Press, 1958. The exceptions occur where I have preferred variant manuscript readings, also noted by Garrod. The text of the letters is that of H. E. Rollins, *The Letters of John Keats, 1814–1821*, 2 vols. Cambridge University Press, 1958, and I have reproduced Keats's punctuation and spelling (though not always his erasures) in accordance with this edition. Brackets thus [ ] are used to indicate dates and words added to make the text intelligible.

I should like to thank W. E. Haxworth for his extremely practical criticism and suggestions, many of which I have adopted; throughout the work on this selection I have received much friendly and constructive guidance from the general editor, James Reeves.

R. G.

INTRODUCTION

1. LIFE

JOHN KEATS was born on 31 October 1795 in London. His mother, Frances, was the daughter of a well-to-do innholder and property-owner, John Jennings; his father, Thomas Keats, had West Country ancestry, and was probably better-connected than has often been said. When John Jennings retired at the end of 1802, Thomas Keats took over the management of one of his properties, the Swan and Hoop inn and stables on London Wall. The lease was due shortly to run out, but whether Thomas Keats intended to take on the business himself will never be known, for in April 1804 he was killed in a riding accident at the early age of thirty, leaving four small children of whom John was the eldest. Faced with financial difficulty, and possessing by all accounts an impulsive temperament, his widow married again in two months. Within another year her own father died, and she and her new husband engaged in an acrimonious lawsuit over the will with her own mother and brother. A year more, and she had separated from her second husband, the children going to live with their grandmother.

All these elements of instability, introduced into Keats's early life, were reflected in his later temperament, the 'horrid morbidity' he recognized in himself. Luckily there was an almost perfect counter-balance in the school where he and his brothers, George and Tom, boarded. Clarke's School at Enfield, ten miles north of London, was ahead of its time in its curriculum and its liberal outlook. Keats found there a freedom of thought and expression, and a feeling for history and the classics unhampered by the out-of-date régime of larger schools. Most important of all for him was the family atmosphere of the school, and with the headmaster's son, Charles Cowden Clarke, he formed a lasting friendship. His volatile character made him far from the conventional good boy; 'always in extremes', he did little work and had a passion for fighting. A dramatic change came at the age of thirteen, it seems likely, after a reconciliation between his mother and grandmother, and the return of the former to live with her children. He now put all his overwhelming energy into work and reading, and won his first prize at midsummer 1809. Another blow, however, was soon to come. His mother's family contained a tendency to tuberculosis, and she herself succumbed in March 1810. During the previous Christmas holidays, the fourteen-year-old boy had taken almost entire charge of her nursing, giving her medicine, reading to her and watching by her all night. His grief when she died was devastating.

That summer he left school and was apprenticed to the family doctor, Thomas Hammond, surgeon, of Edmonton. There is no evidence that this choice of profession was forced on him. It seems, however, that he did not get on personally with Hammond, and that a quarrel caused him to break his terms of residence with him. He spent much of his spare time with Charles Cowden Clarke at Enfield, and was regarded as still in some ways an unofficial pupil. Clarke introduced him late to poetry, but when he did the effect was astonishing. The occasion was a reading of Spenser when Keats was about eighteen; he was utterly carried away by the experience, and produced his first poem, *In Imitation of Spenser*. For the next year or two he experimented, not very successfully, with various poetic models; his passionate intensity concentrated on this, and he told his brothers that if he could not be a poet he would kill himself. He completed his apprenticeship and entered Guy's Hospital on 1 October 1815. His swift promotion to be a dresser there, the equivalent of a junior house-surgeon, was a sign of considerable medical ability, but his fellow-students noticed that poetry now absorbed him. In July 1816, he obtained a licence to practice from the Society of Apothecaries. His grandmother had died, and so had one of the two trustees she had appointed to look after her daughter's children. The remaining trustee, Richard Abbey, a City tea-broker, having spent most of Keats's inheritance from his grandmother on a long and expensive medical training, expected him to set up as a doctor; but events were now moving decisively in the direction of poetry. In May 1816, the poet and editor Leigh Hunt published a sonnet by Keats in his progressive weekly, *The Examiner*, and in the autumn Charles Cowden Clarke showed Hunt more of Keats's poems. An invitation to meet Hunt followed, and by his twenty-first birthday Keats found himself swept into a new and brilliant circle of poets, critics and artists, and had written his own first great poem, *On First Looking into Chapman's Homer*. An article by Hunt on *Young Poets* quoted the poem in full, and, as a fellow-student of Keats said, 'sealed his fate'. He already felt himself temperamentally unsuited for surgery, and he now decided to give up the profession of medicine for ever, outraging the business sense of his ex-trustee. By an ironic twist there was, unknown to them both, a trust fund still in Chancery from the family lawsuit which could have alleviated the money troubles that eroded the rest of Keats's short life. He disguised his difficulties with a careless prodigality, and the wealthy Shelley, who met him at this time, wrote him down as having plenty of money. Other friends were Benjamin Robert Haydon, historical painter and saviour of the Elgin Marbles, J. H. Reynolds, the brilliant parodist, and William Hazlitt, the critic.

Supported by his new friends, and by the fanatical enthusiasm of his brothers, with whom he now lodged in Cheapside, Keats in March 1817 brought out his first *Poems*; but though well-reviewed, it aroused no interest, and the publishers themselves were ashamed of the book. New publishers, the progressive firm of Taylor and Hessey, had more faith, and contracted to print the long poem he had already planned, *Endymion*. Keats wrote this in Hampstead, where he and his brothers had moved, the Isle of Wight, Margate, Canterbury, Hastings, Oxford and Box Hill, spending his last remaining money in the process. He also acquired many new friends, notably Benjamin Bailey, an Oxford undergraduate who deepened his interest in philosophy, and Charles Brown and Charles Wentworth Dilke, who owned the double property in Hampstead named Wentworth Place.

The winter of 1817 to 1818, when he was revising *Endymion*, was full of intense activity for Keats. His letters contain the most profound statements about poets and poetry; his social life included meetings with Wordsworth, which chilled his personal regard for the older poet, though he remained an admirer of his work. He attended Hazlitt's lectures on *The English Poets*, and followed up a suggestion in one of these by writing a narrative poem based on Boccaccio, *Isabella*; *or The Pot of Basil*. Family difficulties returned to cloud his life. Tom Keats showed clearly the family tendency to tuberculosis, while George Keats decided to marry and emigrate to America, though leaving behind some money for Keats to live on. Keats, after nursing Tom during a holiday in Devon, saw George and his wife off from Liverpool, and proceeded on a walking-tour of Scotland with Charles Brown in summer 1818. Part of his plan was to gain inspiration for a new epic poem on the Gods and Titans, *Hyperion*. Meanwhile, there had been signs that the newly published *Endymion* might be attacked because of Keats's association with Leigh Hunt and his so-called 'Cockney School' of poetry. Keats fell ill on tour and returned to Hampstead in August to find Tom obviously dying. In September came the double blow of brutally unfavourable reviews in *Blackwood's Edinburgh Magazine* and *The Quarterly Review*.

Keats was not unduly disturbed by these reviews. 'I think,' he wrote with modest confidence, 'I shall be among the English Poets at my death'; he began his epic *Hyperion*, and continued it throughout the daily tasks of nursing the dying Tom. The isolation he now felt made him specially susceptible to women, the effects of three of whom are fully chronicled in his letters about this time. These were Jane Cox (a cousin of J. H. Reynolds), Isabella Jones, an enigmatic lady with a complicated private life, and Fanny Brawne, a young and attractive Hampstead neighbour. Tom Keats died on 1 December 1818, and Keats went to live with Charles Brown in his portion of Wentworth Place, next door to Dilke. In the New Year, a visit with Brown to relations of Dilke in Chichester and Hampshire sent him off on *The Eve of St. Agnes*, a poem on a popular superstition suggested by Isabella Jones, and perhaps coloured by his growing feelings toward Fanny Brawne. *Hyperion* had broken down, as did a companion piece to *St. Agnes*, another poem with a medieval background, *The Eve of St. Mark*. Keats passed through one of the periods of extreme restlessness and depression which were never far from him, though in them he worked out some of his deepest comments on life. Poetically, this state culminated in the sonnet *On a Dream* and the nightmarelike *La Belle Dame Sans Merci*, both written in April 1819. By then Fanny Brawne and her family lived next door to Keats, the Dilkes having moved, and some understanding had developed between them, though for the penniless Keats there was no hope of an official engagement yet. Nevertheless, the greater calm and happiness this brought him is reflected in the famous Odes he wrote in late April and May; though these face the impermanence of life, they have an underlying serenity that forms a background to their passionate questionings.

Once more material concerns diverted him. His brother George was speculating unwisely in America, and there were doubts whether their shares of the dead Tom's estate would be immediately available. Urged by Charles Brown, Keats planned to make money in two ways. One was to write a popular narrative poem; the other was to try a play in collaboration with Brown. That summer, in the Isle of Wight and at Winchester, Keats wrote the poem, *Lamia*, and the play, *Otho the Great*, which he followed by a much more promising fragment *King Stephen*. He also revised his poems for a new volume, and took up the theme of Hyperion in an entirely new and far more profound way. This huge burst of activity was interrupted by news of financial disaster from George. Keats recovered his serenity sufficiently to write the perfect *To Autumn*, but he too was now heading for disaster. Latent tuberculosis, caught while nursing Tom, was sapping his life; absence from Fanny Brawne made her irresistible when he returned to London in October 1819. Illness and love, though now on the basis of an engagement, brought back his 'morbidity of temperament'. His brother George paid a flying visit in New Year 1820, and left with most of the available family funds. This was probably only a fair squaring of accounts with John, but he appeared to feel it deeply, and early in February a sudden haemorrhage unmistakably announced tuberculosis.

The remaining year of what he was to call his 'posthumous life' was agonizing. The doctors had no real idea of treatment, one even diagnosing that the disease was 'on his *mind*'. Keats's judgement, under stress and illness, was certainly warped, and his letters to Fanny Brawne pass from tender feeling to jealousy (p. 172). At the beginning of July 1820 his *Lamia* was published and attracted favourable reviews, but he was too far gone to take much interest. After further alarming attacks, he was nursed by Fanny Brawne and her widowed mother, and it was decided to send him to winter in Italy. Joseph Severn, his young painter friend, went with him, and they left England in the middle of September. After a voyage which was probably the last blow to his health, they reached Naples and proceeded to Rome, where Dr. James Clark had found them lodgings at 26 Piazza di Spagna. After a brief respite Keats had a massive relapse, and although his immense vitality kept him lingering, he died in Severn's arms on 23 February 1821. He was buried in the Protestant Cemetery, where the epitaph he had requested—'Here lies one whose name was writ in water'—was engraved on his tombstone.

2. POEMS

The most obvious, though by no means the most important aspect of Keats's poetry is its sensuous identification with the objects and situations it describes. This follows from the kind of poet Keats felt himself to be, the 'camelion' (chameleon) faculty he set out in his letter to Richard Woodhouse of 27 October 1818 (p. 87). Contrasting himself with the detached or 'egotistical' type of poet, he defined his poetic process as a complete absorption of his whole being in the object of contemplation, so that he lost his own 'identity' and took on its nature. This idea, to which there are many parallels in his remarks about poets and poetry, gives a tangible awareness to many of his lines so that they seem like a direct experience of the senses. The sensation of sudden movement in

> Ring-doves may fly convuls'd across to some high-cedar'd lair;

of coolness in

> Had felt the cold full sponge to pleasure press'd

of isolated sound in

> The red-breast whistles from a garden-croft

of gloom and sadness in the opening of *Hyperion*

> Deep in the shady sadness of a vale

all strike us as a direct experience, with no intervention from the poet, who transfers these sensuous impressions unaltered to the reader.

Yet this faculty, though it gives a poetic tone of voice and climate to his work, was very far from all that Keats meant to achieve, and in part did achieve in poetry. Merely to transfer, however successfully, the nature of the external world into poetry was not enough. Writing of Byron he said, 'He describes what he sees—I describe what I imagine—Mine is the hardest task.' On the one hand he believed that what he called 'A Man of Achievement, especially in Literature' must possess this '*Negative Capability*, that is, when a man is capable of being in uncertainties, mysteries, doubts, without any irritable searching after fact and reason', the philosophic counterpart of the passive receptiveness of the poet. On the other hand, he believed that an active exercise of the imagination by the poet could actually create truth; he uses a strongly active verb for this process. 'What the Imagination seizes as Beauty must be truth—whether it existed before or not—' (p. 37), and he goes on to assert that imagination can create reality, as Adam dreamt of Eve before she was created. 'The Imagination may be compared to Adam's dream —he awoke and found it truth.' He did not believe that, for him,

7

this truth could be approached by 'consequitive' reasoning, and he did not believe it was part of the poetic process to reason in verse. What marks out his poems is their endeavour to make something new, 'whether it existed before or not'. The poet, without being any less of a philosopher, is a maker whose thought is poetry.

At their best, the poems of Keats have this quality of being absolute creations in their own right. The world of the *Ode to a Nightingale* did not exist before he wrote it, and it now exists for ever. The Odes generally, the two unfinished Hyperion poems and some shorter pieces have this authority of unique creation; yet Keats was the first to feel dissatisfied with his achievement as a poet compared with his idea of it. He even moved on to the idea, present from quite an early stage in his mind, that even poetry itself at the highest was 'not so fine a thing' as philosophy and the good life. Yet until illness made creative work impossible, he showed no sign, as has sometimes been said, of regarding his poetic career as done. Part of the interest in looking at his brief packed life of poetry is to see it as a continuous attempt to make himself more and more effective as a poet. Owing to his concentrated energy, it is possible to see in three years, from autumn 1816 to autumn 1819, a growth and change which in many writers is spread over most of a lifetime. It is a supremely conscious attempt to fit himself for the life of a poet, and everything, experience, thought and reading was used for this end.

His poems therefore show a continuous progression of both ideas and techniques, some deliberate and many unconscious. In his passive capacity he was swept up in every new influence; as an active creator, he tried to shape each one to his notion of poetry. Discounting most of the purely imitative work of his two first years of writing—summer 1814 to summer 1816—his poems are all written in a way that follows these two aspects of his poetic nature. Unlike most poets, whose method of composition fits better with Wordsworth's doctrine of 'emotion recollected in tranquillity', Keats's writing is an almost instant transmutation of impressions, thoughts, reading and ideas into poetry. It follows that his life is

8

closely connected with his work, and that, as one of his publishers noticed, there is a great deal of reality in everything he writes. On the other hand, his powers of imagination are so strong, that the poems are far from being a poetic diary of the life, and enrich their original impulse with a complete life of their own. As a concrete case of this process, a chance visit to a dedication service at Stansted Chapel in January 1819 clearly led Keats to his famous description of the stained glass windows in *The Eve of St. Agnes* and of the illuminated manuscript in *The Eve of St. Mark*, both written within a few weeks of the event; yet his creation outdoes the original in detail, atmosphere and concentrated imagery so as to become something entirely his own. This was, moreover, a deliberate process; he looked at beautiful or striking scenery, as he himself said, 'for poetical purposes' and he regarded most of his day-by-day reading as 'study' for poetry.

The work of his three great years shows an increasing mastery of impressions and influences as his own technique, by constant self-criticism and practice, grew more and more assured. His early reading of Spenser's *The Faerie Queene*, and the teaching of Charles Cowden Clarke 'that epic was of all the king' gave him the slightly false idea, which he defended while writing *Endymion*, that a great poem had to be a long poem. His early writings are full of plans for these large-scale works, which in the end he found burdensome, growing tired of *Endymion* before he had completed it, and leaving both versions of *Hyperion* unfinished. Yet his tendency to write at length, which weakens much of his early poetry, was a wonderful poetic training. *Endymion* itself, written over several months in 1817, is a loose allegory of a young man's search for love and of a poet's search for truth, coming to the typically Keatsian conclusion that both can only be found by embracing experience and reality, not by avoiding them. The importance of its rather vague scope—'I must make 4000 Lines of one bare circumstance and fill them with Poetry'—was that it enabled Keats to find a way of thinking about the problems of his own life in poetry, notably in the passage in Book One beginning 'Wherein lies happiness?' and that in Book

9

Four beginning 'There lies a den' (pp. 32 and 38). It is an exploration of the poet's soul in a way reminiscent of Wordsworth's *The Prelude*, and though Keats, of course, never saw that poem, he was already far ahead of most critics of his time in his appreciation of the older poet, whose *The Excursion* he judged one of the finest things of the age.

Meanwhile in shorter poems, notably in sonnet form, Keats had reached a maturity and depth of expression. His next large work, *Isabella; or The Pot of Basil*, marks a transition, an attempt to write a rounded story and not lose the freedom of poetical thought in the process. These two are at war in this poem, which often seems a romantic tale in verse, like Leigh Hunt's *The Story of Rimini*, interrupted by philosophic digressions. In it Keats reverts to some of the worst features of his association with Hunt, which by this time (spring 1818) he had outgrown in fact, and there is a cosiness and coyness which he himself soon condemned as 'mawkish'. His eye, in fact, was already on what he felt to be a more serious attempt to write a great philosophic poem, *Hyperion*, using the myth of the older Titans dispossessed by the younger gods as an allegory of evolution and particularly the evolution of poetry, in the dispossession of Hyperion by Apollo. Encouraged by his academic friend Bailey, he prepared himself for this by a study of epic verse, *The Excursion*, *Paradise Lost* and *The Inferno* in translation, and by plunging himself into epic scenery on his walking-tour of the Lakes and Scotland. His mastery of technique through his previous large-scale writing is fulfilled in this poem, which though unfinished—it breaks off in the middle of Book Three with Apollo's assumption of godhead—was recognized even by his opponents as a supreme achievement. It was also deepened by the tragic circumstances of his own life, which dominated the year of extraordinary creative activity begun by this poem (September 1818 to September 1819).

In this year, each major poem may be regarded as a stepping-stone to another. The richness and concentration of his writing of *Hyperion* not only marks out that poem; it has its reward when he turns to a romantic narrative, *The Eve of St. Agnes*, a poem which creates a world of sensuous impression, colour and young love, and carries off a successful narrative line without ever once flagging in invention and technique. His brief burst of ' Gothic' poems—*St. Agnes*, *St. Mark* and *La Belle Dame Sans Merci*—in the early months of 1819 themselves sent him back to the more restrained sonnet form. Dissatisfied with this, now that his powers had developed toward a more complex form of expression, he evolved out of experiments with the sonnet a new form, that of the major Odes. These embody the strength and weight of *Hyperion* with the dramatic flow of *St. Agnes*; they are as concentrated as his sonnets, but able to sustain their ideas through several stanzas. His sense of the music of words, the linking assonance within lines and from line to line here find their highest expression. In the Odes, Keats has found a tone of voice for thinking aloud in verse. They are great Socratic discussions carried on with himself about the meaning and purpose of life, and the verse, formal yet flexible, is fitted to maintain every turn and question of his meditations.

At the same time he developed for narrative a new technique based on an intense study of Dryden's couplets. He used this in *Lamia*, a poem which he wished to bring more in line with real life than his previous narratives had been. He tried to make this form carry every nuance of human experience, descriptive, passionate, philosophic and satirical. He was working toward a method that, he felt, would be adapted to the complex matter he now felt life to be, a feeling deepened as his own engagement with life and death became more and more complicated. He also experimented, uneasily at first though with growing certainty and interest, in purely dramatic writing, but his chief attempt was to revise and re-write *Hyperion*, which he had broken off in the spring, along entirely different lines. Instead of making it entirely objective, a detached allegory of the poetic life, he now felt the need to make it openly a record of his own poetic nature, and to introduce himself into it as Dante had introduced himself into *The Inferno*, on which the remodelled fragment is largely based. In thus writing 'frankly about himself and about poetry', as one critic has said, he moves into a new form of expression, whose ease and clarity is also reflected in the last of the Odes he wrote at this time, *To Autumn*.

Keats therefore was continuously experimenting and developing right up to the end of his writing life. Even the one considerable work after his great year, the comic poem *The Cap and Bells*, written in the winter of 1819–20 up to the time of his physical breakdown, is an attempt, though largely abortive, to find a poetry that would express all sides of human life, including satire and humour. In finding ways of poetic expression for his own phenomenal growth of experience and thought, he struck off poems as he himself said of Shakespeare 'full of fine things said unintentionally'. Yet he never wasted an idea or a phrase, and a study of his working manuscripts shows how, in his own words to Shelley, he formed the habit of loading every rift of his subject with ore. He hardly ever allowed a poem to go cold on him, and he hardly ever abandoned an idea or expression in one part of a poem without managing to insert it in another. His excitement, curiosity and interest in writing a poem communicates itself to the reader even where his expression falls short of his intention, and partly explains why his poems find favour even with critics who have rejected much of the work of his contemporaries.

3. LETTERS

Keats's letters, which seemed to many critics of the last century to be unworthy of publication, and even to detract from his genius, are now studied almost as closely as his poems themselves. Their prime interest for modern critics is the light they throw on the composition of poetry and on aesthetic theory. T. S. Eliot wrote

> There is hardly one statement of Keats about poetry, which, when considered carefully and with due allowance for the difficulties of communication, will not be found to be true: and what is more, true for greater and more mature poetry than anything Keats ever wrote.

In this category come his pronouncements on Negative Capability, on the nature of the 'camelion' poet, the axioms of poetic composition he expressed to his publisher, and taken together with many less-formed remarks they compose a large and fairly coherent body of thought. When inconsistencies are found, it should be remembered that Keats scribbled all these remarks, without thought of future analysis, in his day-by-day letters to friends and relations. Why they remain so generally valid is because Keats probably thought more continually about poetry than any of his contemporaries. Whereas Coleridge, Wordsworth and Shelley could be diverted into metaphysics, politics and science, Keats thought and wrote with boundless interest about literature and literary composition. Moreover, he 'never sophisticated'; his ideas spring from genuine reactions, unaffected by fashion. Perhaps the only criticism would be that he is unusually hard on the 'literary fashionables' of his day, notably Byron. In some instances he is far ahead of his time; his criticism of Wordsworth is outstanding in both its justice and general appreciation.

Another interesting side to the letters is the light they throw on the background and thought of his own composition. It becomes more and more clear, as the letters are studied, that an incident, idea or expression from the letters anticipates or coincides with a poem that he writes. His philosophic remarks on 'the vale of Soul-making' in April anticipate the great Odes of summer 1819, and the description of his daily walk at Winchester later that year is almost literally transcribed in part of his *To Autumn*. Poems in their first draft occur frequently in his letters, so that the prose description and the poetic counterpart flow naturally into each other, as in the sonnet *On a Dream*. Particularly in the region of philosophy, the mature position of the letters is often several months ahead of its expression in the poems; the growth of his poetic mind was often faster than the growth of his poetic technique, and the poems sometimes grope toward ideas that have been memorably set out in an earlier letter.

It must not be thought, however, that the letters are only interesting as a repository of aesthetic and poetic ideas, a professional working notebook. Keats had an intense feeling for what seemed to him essential and real in human existence; 'I am more at home,'

13

he remarked, 'amongst Men and Women.' The many friends that he acquired, their characters, their relationships, their reactions to him and to each other are portrayed with a vivid truth that makes these people, some of them quite unremarkable by other standards, live and breathe still as if they were our contemporaries as well as his. His appreciation of their idiosyncracies has generally a charity and an understanding that seems quite Shakespearian. 'Men should bear with each other,' he wrote, 'there lives not the Man who may not be cut up, aye hashed to pieces on his weakest side'. In his own circle, this chance collection of lawyers, civil servants and middle-class professional men, he discerned how each one tapped some individual spring of human nature. The brilliant ephemeral Reynolds, the serious and sometimes obtuse Bailey, Charles Brown, coarse yet kindly, the over-anxious and dogmatic Dilke all receive a treatment that insures our future knowledge of them in a way that Keats could not have anticipated. Often their character is displayed through Keats's enjoyment of some entirely trivial incident, as with this, of Reynolds:

I must tell you a good thing Reynolds *did*: 'twas the best thing he ever *said*. You know that at taking leave of a party at a door way, sometimes a Man dallies and foolishes and gets awkward, and does not know how to make off to advantage—Good bye—well—good-bye—and yet he does not go—good bye and so on—well—good bless you—You know what I mean. Now Reynolds was in this predicament and got out of it in a very witty way. He was leaving us at Hampstead. He delay'd, and we were joking at him and even said, 'be off'—at which he put the tails of his coat between his legs, and sneak'd off as nigh like a spanial as could be. He went with flying colours: this is very clever—

Nor are such passages merely pen-portraits of individuals. They form a unique picture of a little-known section of Regency society. In a time fully documented by diaries and memoirs in the field of political and fashionable life, Keats's letters fill a gap in our understanding of the lives of the energetic, intelligent middle-class. Their habits, customs, even their vulgarities are brought vividly before us. This is specially valuable since the era that followed changed so much that had been for so long native to England. It was an age when conversation and manners could still be compared, as Keats's friend B. R. Haydon compared them, with those of Shakespeare's day. Keats continually gives us insight into the daily life and habits of this level of society. At the same time, although he records contemporary manners, he always judged with detachment what was merely fashionable and temporary. He writes of the wit-circle of Horace Smith the parodist, and their criticism of Edmund Kean the actor:

> They only served to convince me, how superior humour is to wit in respect to enjoyment—These men say things that make one start, without making one feel, they are all alike; their manners are alike; they all know fashionables, they have a mannerism in their very eating & drinking, in their mere handling a Decanter—They talked of Kean & his low company —Would I were with that company instead of yours said I to myself!

All this is presented in a prose style that matches the times and his themes. If it resembles his favourite eighteenth-century novelists, Fielding, Smollett and Sterne, and sometimes borrows from his favourite contemporary prose-writer, William Hazlitt, it is one more reminder how, for Keats, life and literature were part of each other. His prose too has a dramatic quality like some of the great set speeches in Shakespeare, and reminds us what a playwright he might have been. Indeed, in what he and his friends called his 'rhodomontades', talking or writing to effect an impression, he plays with and develops a theme in a way half-humorous, half-serious that is entirely his own. Even if this is full of monstrous exaggeration, as in his diatribe against Parsons (itself an echo of Hazlitt's essays *On the Clerical Character*) he always lets us know that he himself is aware of the exaggeration:

> A Parson is a Lamb in a drawing room and a lion in a Vestry—The notions of Society will not permit a Parson to give way to his temper in any shape—so he festers in himself—his features get a peculiar diabolical self sufficient iron stupid expression—He is continually acting—His mind

is against every Man and every Mans mind is against him—He is an Hippocrite to the Believer and a Coward to the unbeliever—He must be either a Knave or an Ideot—And there is no Man so much to be pitied as an ideot parson—The soldier who is cheated into an esprit de corps—by a red coat, a Band and Colours for the purpose of nothing—is not half so pitiable as the Parson who is led by the nose by the Bench of Bishops—and is smothered in absurdities—a poor necessary subaltern of the Church—

In the end, in spite of these fascinating by-products, we read the letters of Keats primarily because they tell us so much about Keats himself, and bring us so close to him as a person. They are a great discourse in which he ranges over nearly every aspect of his life. There are very few areas of non-communication, though these are significant. He is almost totally silent about his parents and child-hood, and money-questions are among the few matters that seem to make him embarrassed or evasive; both these points are easily explained by his early history. These apart, his letters are an almost entirely unselfconscious stream of consciousness. In these letters Keats analyses himself in every situation in a way that helps to explain his splendid sanity in a life of extreme stress. He is supremely conscious of his own nature, and it is clear that much of this letter-writing, often far into the night, and the impromptu and impulsive poems that sprinkle its pages, were a kind of therapy for his com-plicated spirit. 'Sane I went to bed and sane I arose', he remarked after one profound piece of writing in both prose and poetry. He was fully aware of his own weak spots both in art and in conduct. 'My own domestic criticism,' he wrote to his publisher, 'has given me pain without comparison beyond what Blackwood or the Quarterly could possibly inflict.' In his own personality he realized that there were knots, such as his attitude toward women, 'which must take time to unravell and care to keep unravelled'. In spite of his vitality, sense of fun and animal spirits, his personal view of life was tragic and heroic, but at the same time positive. Faced with the contradictions of his own nature and history, which he saw every-where repeated in life around him, Keats believed that he should continuously try to find an answer; he did not minimize but he continually attacked the problem. As Lionel Trilling has said:

> It is in terms of the self-confronting hostile or painful circumstance that Keats make his magnificent effort at the solution of the problem of evil, his heroic attempt to show how it is that life may be called blessed when its circumstances are cursed.

In this sense many of his most profound letters are not written *to* anyone; he is using correspondence as a kind of spiritual journal. This is particularly true of the long journal letters he wrote to his brother George in 1818–19, when the latter had emigrated. On the other hand, he was always responsive to any special need in those who received his letters. Realizing the loneliness of his young sister Fanny, who suffered from the oppressive guardianship of Abbey, he set out to write her a regular series of letters, roughly every fortnight. These, by a lucky chance the only fairly complete set of letters still in England, show how well and sympathetically he could write, without a trace of writing-down, to one whose character, as he said, was not formed.

As illness overwhelmed him in his last year, his tragic view of life often grew obsessive, and the heroism of his healthy self frequently gave way to morbid despairs. The publication, in the 1870s, of many letters to Fanny Brawne dating from this period, gave emphasis to this phase in his life, and caused unfavourable comment at the time. Yet even these only show how great an innate sense of the tragic Keats had always to contend with, and how successfully, when control was not loosened by illness, he managed to meet it, and even turn it to good. His conviction was that life should be faced and its difficulties put to use—'lord! a man should have the fine point of his soul taken off to become fit for this world'. We read his letters for encouragement, though not for escape, and his life, so generously and modestly displayed in them, helps us to enlarge our own.

4. POSITION AND REPUTATION AS A POET

Keats's writing life (1814–20) came at a crucial point in the history of English poetry. The previous century had been dominated by the Augustan or classical school, based on the poetry of Pope and the criticism of Dr. Johnson, having more in common with French poetry than with any other English verse since Chaucer. The first wave of English 'Romantic' poets, William Wordsworth and Samuel Taylor Coleridge, had issued the uncompromising manifesto of a new style, their *Lyrical Ballads*, in 1798, and were now both in their forties. Orthodox criticism had had time to turn its guns on them, and their reputation was probably at its lowest ebb. Wordsworth was allowed some credit as a philosopher of a kind of Christian pantheism, but when his philosophic poem *The Excursion* appeared in 1814 it was mostly reviewed adversely; Coleridge was treated with even more suspicion, and his poems were generally mocked as unintelligible.

Keats's own early taste was modelled on the conventional reading of Cowden Clarke, but his attitude to the poetic controversy of the day was first of all based on Leigh Hunt's *The Examiner*, which he started reading as a schoolboy. Hunt continually attacked the Augustan or 'French' school, but he was also fashionably unfair to Wordsworth and Coleridge, whom he dismissed without troubling to read their works, which he assumed to be crude and commonplace. This double attitude was echoed exactly by Keats in *Sleep and Poetry* (1816), where he first attacked the Augustans for forgetting the tradition of English poetry:

> Could all this be forgotten? Yes, a schism
> Nurtured by foppery and barbarism,
> Made great Apollo blush for this his land.
> Men were thought wise who could not understand
> His glories: with a puling infant's force
> They sway'd about upon a rocking horse,
> And thought it Pegasus.

The last phrase exactly echoed an article in *The Examiner* by Hazlitt on Milton's versification:

> Dr. Johnson and Pope would have converted his (Milton's) Pegasus into a rocking-horse.

Keats, however, did not proceed to hail the first wave of Romanticism, but again echoed *The Examiner* in his cautious estimate of the new poetry of Wordsworth and Coleridge, which he characterized as

> Strange thunders from the potency of song;
> Mingled indeed with what is clear and strong,
> From majesty; but in clear truth the themes
> Are ugly clubs, the Poets Polyphemes
> Disturbing the grand sea.

These passages of attempted criticism had the most unfortunate consequences for Keats. His comment on Pope brought on him all the invective of Lord Byron, romantic in his themes but severely classical in his taste and technique; his remarks on the new poetry cannot have commended him to Wordsworth, whom he came increasingly to admire with wider reading in his work. Worst of all, they announced him a supporter of the middle way of mild and sentimental romanticism advocated and practised by Leigh Hunt. Keats outwore this phase in a few months, but its publicly expressed reputation dogged him, and formed the basis for the attacks on his own poetry in *Blackwood's* and *The Quarterly*. The worst of every school of poetry was therefore attributed to him in his lifetime. He found himself reckoned to be as obscure as the earlier Romantics, but without their philosophy, to be as affected and quaint as Leigh Hunt, and to be writing couplets as Pope had done but without understanding the first principles of their versification. Even his literary friends did him disservice by concentrating their praise on the lushness and what they called the 'beauties' of his verse.

This situation led to two myths, both of which partly vitiated his reputation for many years after his death. One was that put out by hostile reviewers, the affected and silly 'Johnny Keats' invented by *Blackwood's*, the 'Cockney' imitator of Leigh Hunt; the other was the picture painted by Shelley in his *Adonais* of a fragile and hypersensitive genius killed by the reviewers. These false views of Keats's personality coloured the popular idea of his poetry, which was thought by the uninformed Victorian reader to be full of mild sentiment and luxuriant fancy, even if these were then regarded as terms of praise.

Even though it was often on such false terms as these, the growth of Keats's reputation in the first half of the nineteenth century was steady and remarkable. There were three main aids to his popularity. The first was his championship by the young Cambridge society called The Apostles, one of whom, Tennyson, was writing Keatsian poetry in the 1830s, and drawing down on himself the same vulgar attacks from the same critics. The second, in the next decade, was the canonisation of his verse by the Pre-Raphaelite Brotherhood of painters, who found his poems, particularly *The Eve of St. Agnes*, *Isabella* and *La Belle Dame Sans Merci*, a prime source of inspiration. Thirdly, there was always a small but genuine appreciation of his character and work, summed up by his own brother's remark that he was 'as much like the *holy ghost* as *Johnny Keats*'. Among poets, the long-lived W. S. Landor was certainly influenced by him. In 1848, the long-delayed *Life, Letters, and Literary Remains, of John Keats*, edited by Richard Monckton Milnes, seemed to set the seal upon his reputation. In point of fact, its Victorianism gave longer life to some of the false impressions, so that as late as 1870, a female critic could write of 'The Daintiest of Poets—Keats'. He was also confused with the 'art for art's sake' of Swinburne, Rossetti and Morris. Even Arnold thought him led astray by his admiration for the luxuriant images of the Elizabethans. At best, he was still regarded as a poet's poet.

The last quarter of the nineteenth century saw Keats's reputation for 'daintiness' take a toss from the publication of his outspoken letters to Fanny Brawne (see p. 172), and, in our own century, appreciation began to be based on his real qualities of strong thought, direct apprehension of beauty and vivid concrete imagery.

He was still the inspiration of poets, and the war-poet Wilfred Owen kept his death-date as a virtual day of mourning, so close was his identification with him; but his forthright and human philosophy was now reaching a wider audience, who saw the connection between the letters of Keats and his poems. His universality has won approval from critics as diverse as A. C. Bradley, John Middleton Murry, Lytton Strachey, T. S. Eliot, F. R. Leavis, and the 'New Critics' of American scholarship, and his reputation has suffered none of the eclipses that many of his contemporaries, such as Shelley, have experienced. Poets as individually eminent as W. B. Yeats have echoed him in their greatest work, and his present position, both as a poet and as a thinker and writer about poetry, stands as high as at any time in the 150-odd years since his death.

SUGGESTIONS FOR FURTHER READING

1. POEMS

   The Poems of John Keats, ed. Ernest de Selincourt (Methuen, revised 1926, reprinted 1954).

   The Poetical Works of John Keats, ed. H. W. Garrod (Oxford, 2nd edition, 1958).

2. LETTERS

   The Letters of John Keats, 1814–1821, ed. H. E. Rollins (Cambridge, Mass., and C.U.P., 1958), 2 vols.

   The Keats Circle, Letters and Papers, 1816–1878, ed. H. E. Rollins (Cambridge, Mass., and O.U.P., 1948), 2 vols.

3. BIOGRAPHY, CRITICISM, ETC.

   Walter Jackson Bate, *John Keats* (Cambridge, Mass., and O.U.P., 1963).

   Robert Gittings, *John Keats*, (Heinemann 1968).

   Robert Gittings, *John Keats: The Living Year* (Heinemann, 1954).

   D. G. James, *The Romantic Comedy* (O.U.P., 1948), Part II, 'Purgatory Blind'.

   John Middleton Murry, *Keats and Shakespeare* (O.U.P., 1925).

   M. R. Ridley, *Keats' Craftsmanship* (Methuen, 1933, reprinted University Paperbacks 1963).

   Lionel Trilling, *The Opposing Self* (Secker & Warburg, 1955). First Essay, 'The Poet as Hero: Keats in his Letters'.

   Aileen Ward, *John Keats: The Making of a Poet* (Secker & Warburg, 1963).

Extract from

I stood tip-toe upon a little hill

LINGER awhile upon some bending planks   61
That lean against a streamlet's rushy banks,
And watch intently Nature's gentle doings:
They will be found softer than ring-dove's cooings.
How silent comes the water round that bend;
Not the minutest whisper does it send
To the o'er hanging sallows: blades of grass
Slowly across the chequer'd shadows pass.
Why, you might read two sonnets, ere they reach
To where the hurrying freshnesses aye preach   70
A natural sermon o'er their pebbly beds;
Where swarms of minnows show their little heads,
Staying their wavy bodies 'gainst the streams,
To taste the luxury of sunny beams
Temper'd with coolness. How they ever wrestle
With their own sweet delight, and ever nestle
Their silver bellies on the pebbly sand.
If you but scantily hold out the hand,
That very instant not one will remain;
But turn your eye, and they are there again.   80
The ripples seem right glad to reach those cresses,
And cool themselves among the em'rald tresses;
The while they cool themselves, they freshness give,
And moisture, that the bowery green may live:
So keeping up an interchange of favours,
Like good men in the truth of their behaviours.
Sometimes goldfinches one by one will drop
From low hung branches: little space they stop;

But sip, and twitter, and their feathers sleek;
Then off at once, as in a wanton freak: 90
Or perhaps, to show their black, and golden wings,
Pausing upon their yellow flutterings.

To CHARLES COWDEN CLARKE
Wednesday 9 Oct. [*1816*]
My dear Sir,

The busy time has just gone by, and I can now devote any time you may mention to the pleasure of seeing Mr Hunt—'t will be an Era in my existence—I am anxious too to see the Author of the Sonnet to the Sun, for it is no mean gratification to become acquainted with Men who in their admiration of Poetry do not jumble together Shakspeare and Darwin—I have coppied out a sheet or two of Verses which I composed some time ago, and find
worst
so much to blame in them that the best part will go into the fire—those to G. Mathew I will suffer to meet the eye of Mr H. not withstanding that the Muse is so frequently mentioned. I here sinned in the face of Heaven even while rememb[e]ring what, I think, Horace says, "never presume to make a God appear but for an Action worthy of a God. From a few Words of yours when last I saw you, I have no doubt but that you have something in your Portfolio which I should by rights see—I will put you in Mind of it—Although the Borough is a beastly place in dirt, turnings and windings; yet No 8 Dean Street is not difficult to find; and if you would run the Gauntlet over London Bridge, take the first turning to the left and then the first to the right and moreover knock at my door which is nearly opposite a Meeting, you would do one a Charity which as St Paul saith is the father of all the Virtues—At all events let me hear from you soon—I say at all events not excepting the Gout in your fingers—

Your's Sincerely
John Keats—

24

On first looking into Chapman's Homer

MUCH have I travell'd in the realms of gold,
   And many goodly states and kingdoms seen;
   Round many western islands have I been
Which bards in fealty to Apollo hold.
Oft of one wide expanse had I been told
   That deep-brow'd Homer ruled as his demesne;
   Yet did I never breathe its pure serene
Till I heard Chapman speak out loud and bold:
Then felt I like some watcher of the skies
   When a new planet swims into his ken;   10
Or like stout Cortez when with eagle eyes
   He star'd at the Pacific—and all his men
Look'd at each other with a wild surmise—
   Silent, upon a peak in Darien.

Keen, fitful gusts

KEEN, fitful gusts are whisp'ring here and there
   Among the bushes half leafless, and dry;
   The stars look very cold about the sky,
And I have many miles on foot to fare.
Yet feel I little of the cool bleak air,
   Or of the dead leaves rustling drearily,
   Or of those silver lamps that burn on high,
Or of the distance from home's pleasant lair:
For I am brimfull of the friendliness
   That in a little cottage I have found;   10

Of fair-hair'd Milton's eloquent distress,
  And all his love for gentle Lycid drown'd;
Of lovely Laura in her light green dress,
  And faithful Petrarch gloriously crown'd.

To my Brothers

SMALL, busy flames play through the fresh laid coals,
  And their faint cracklings o'er our silence creep
  Like whispers of the household gods that keep
A gentle empire o'er fraternal souls.
And while, for rhymes, I search around the poles,
  Your eyes are fix'd, as in poetic sleep,
  Upon the lore so voluble and deep,
That aye at fall of night our care condoles.
This is your birth-day Tom, and I rejoice
  That thus it passes smoothly, quietly.   10
Many such eves of gently whisp'ring noise
  May we together pass, and calmly try
What are this world's true joys,—ere the great voice,
  From its fair face, shall bid our spirits fly.

To Haydon

GREAT spirits now on earth are sojourning;
  He of the cloud, the cataract, the lake,
Who on Helvellyn's summit, wide awake,
Catches his freshness from Archangel's wing:
He of the rose, the violet, the spring,
  The social smile, the chain for Freedom's sake:
  And lo!—whose stedfastness would never take

A meaner sound than Raphael's whispering.
And other spirits there are standing apart
   Upon the forehead of the age to come;   10
These, these will give the world another heart,
   And other pulses. Hear ye not the hum
Of mighty workings?—
   Listen awhile ye nations, and be dumb.

On the Grasshopper and the Cricket

THE poetry of earth is never dead:
   When all the birds are faint with the hot sun,
   And hide in cooling trees, a voice will run
From hedge to hedge about the new-mown mead;
That is the Grasshopper's—he takes the lead
   In summer luxury,—he has never done
   With his delights; for when tired out with fun
He rests at ease beneath some pleasant weed.
The poetry of earth is ceasing never:
   On a lone winter evening, when the frost   10
   Has wrought a silence, from the stove there shrills
The Cricket's song, in warmth increasing ever,
   And seems to one in drowsiness half lost,
   The Grasshopper's among some grassy hills.

To JOHN HAMILTON REYNOLDS
Thursday 17 April [1817]

Carisbrooke April 17th

My dear Reynolds,

Ever since I wrote to my Brothers from Southampton I have been in a taking, and at this moment I am about to become settled, for I have unpacked my books, put them into a snug corner—pinned up Haydon—Mary Queen [of] Scotts, and Milton with his daughters in a row. In the passage I found a head of Shakspeare which I had not before seen—It is most likely the same that George spoke so well of; for I like it extremely—Well—this head I have hung over my Books, just above the three in a row, having first discarded a french Ambassador—Now this alone is a good morning's work. Yesterday I went to Shanklin, which occasioned a great debate in my mind whether I should live there or at Carisbrooke. Shanklin is a most beautiful place—sloping wood and meadow ground reaches round the Chine, which is a cleft between the Cliffs of the depth of nearly 300 feet at least. This cleft is filled with trees & bushes in the narrow part; and as it widens becomes bare, if it were not for primroses on one side, which spread to the very verge of the Sea, and some fishermen's huts on the other, perched midway in the Ballustrades of beautiful green Hedges along their steps down to the sands.—But the sea, Jack, the sea—the little waterfall—then the white cliff—then St. Catherine's Hill—"the sheep in the meadows, the cows in the corn."—Then, why are you at Carisbrooke? say you—Because, in the first place, I sho^d be at twice the Expense, and three times the inconvenience—next that from here I can see your continent—from a little hill close by, the whole north Angle of the Isle of Wight, with the water between us. In the 3^d place, I see Carisbrooke Castle from my window, and have found several delightful wood-alleys, and copses, and quick freshes—As for Primroses—the Island ought to be called Primrose Island: that is, if the nation of Cowslips agree thereto, of which there are diverse Clans just beginning to lift up their heads and if an how the Rain holds whereby that is Birds eyes abate—another reason of my fixing is that I am more in reach of the places around me—I intend to walk over the island east—West—North South—I have not seen many specimens of Ruins—I dont think however I shall ever see one to surpass Carisbrooke Castle. The trench is o'ergrown with the smoothest turf, and the Walls with ivy—The Keep within side is one Bower of ivy—a Colony of Jackdaws have been there many years—I dare say I have seen many a descendant of some old cawer who peeped through the Bars at Charles the first, when he was there in Confinement. On the road from Cowes to Newport I saw some extensive Barracks which disgusted me extremely with Government for placing such a Nest of Debauchery in so beautiful a place—I asked a man on the Coach about this—and he said that the people had been spoiled—In the room where I slept at Newport I found this on the Window "O Isle spoilt by the Milatary!"—I must in honesty however confess that I did not feel very sorry at the idea of the Women being a little profligate—The Wind is in a sulky fit, and I feel that it would be no bad thing to be the favorite of some Fairy, who would give one the power of seeing how our Friends got on, at a Distance—I should like, of all Loves, a sketch of you and Tom and George in ink which Haydon will do if you tell him how I want them—From want of regular rest, I have been rather *narvus*—and the passage in Lear—"Do you not hear the Sea?"—has haunted me intensely. . . .

On the Sea

It keeps eternal whisperings around
   Desolate shores, and with its mighty swell
   Gluts twice ten thousand caverns, till the spell
Of Hecate leaves them their old shadowy sound.

Often 'tis in such gentle temper found,
    That scarcely will the very smallest shell
    Be moved for days from where it sometime fell,
When last the winds of heaven were unbound.
Oh ye! who have your eye-balls vexed and tired,
    Feast them upon the wideness of the Sea;   10
    Oh ye! whose ears are dinn'd with uproar rude,
Or fed too much with cloying melody,—
    Sit ye near some old cavern's mouth, and brood
Until ye start, as if the sea-nymphs quired!

Extracts from

Endymion

BOOK I. LINES 232–306

'O THOU, whose mighty palace roof doth hang
From jagged trunks, and overshadoweth
Eternal whispers, glooms, the birth, life, death
Of unseen flowers in heavy peacefulness;
Who lov'st to see the hamadryads dress
Their ruffled locks where meeting hazels darken;
And through whole solemn hours dost sit, and hearken
The dreary melody of bedded reeds—
In desolate places, where dank moisture breeds   240
The pipy hemlock to strange overgrowth;
Bethinking thee, how melancholy loth
Thou wast to lose fair Syrinx—do thou now,
By thy love's milky brow!
By all the trembling mazes that she ran,
Hear us, great Pan!

'O thou, for whose soul-soothing quiet, turtles
Passion their voices cooingly 'mong myrtles,
What time thou wanderest at eventide
Through sunny meadows, that outskirt the side   250
Of thine enmossed realms: O thou, to whom
Broad leaved fig trees even now foredoom
Their ripen'd fruitage; yellow girted bees
Their golden honeycombs; our village leas
Their fairest blossom'd beans and poppied corn;
The chuckling linnet its five young unborn,
To sing for thee; low creeping strawberries
Their summer coolness; pent up butterflies
Their freckled wings; yea, the fresh budding year
All its completions—be quickly near,   260
By every wind that nods the mountain pine,
O forester divine!

'Thou, to whom every faun and satyr flies
For willing service; whether to surprise
The squatted hare while in half sleeping fit;
Or upward ragged precipices flit
To save poor lambkins from the eagle's maw;
Or by mysterious enticement draw
Bewildered shepherds to their path again;
Or to tread breathless round the frothy main,   270
And gather up all fancifullest shells
For thee to tumble into Naiads' cells,
And, being hidden, laugh at their out-peeping;
Or to delight thee with fantastic leaping,
The while they pelt each other on the crown
With silvery oak apples, and fir cones brown—
By all the echoes that about thee ring,
Hear us, O satyr king!

'O Hearkener to the loud clapping shears,
While ever and anon to his shorn peers   280

31

A ram goes bleating: Winder of the horn,
When snouted wild-boars routing tender corn
Anger our huntsmen: Breather round our farms,
To keep off mildews, and all weather harms:
Strange ministrant of undescribed sounds,
That come a swooning over hollow grounds,
And wither drearily on barren moors:
Dread opener of the mysterious doors
Leading to universal knowledge—see,
Great son of Dryope,   290
The many that are come to pay their vows
With leaves about their brows!

   'Be still the unimaginable lodge
For solitary thinkings; such as dodge
Conception to the very bourne of heaven,
Then leave the naked brain: be still the leaven,
That spreading in this dull and clodded earth
Gives it a touch ethereal—a new birth:
Be still a symbol of immensity;
A firmament reflected in a sea;   300
An element filling the space between;
An unknown—but no more: we humbly screen
With uplift hands our foreheads, lowly bending,
And giving out a shout most heaven rending,
Conjure thee to receive our humble Paean,
Upon thy Mount Lycean!'

BOOK I LINES 777–842

Wherein lies happiness? In that which becks
Our ready minds to fellowship divine,
A fellowship with essence; till we shine,
Full alchemiz'd, and free of space. Behold   780
The clear religion of heaven! Fold

A rose leaf round thy finger's taperness,
And soothe thy lips: hist, when the airy stress
Of music's kiss impregnates the free winds,
And with a sympathetic touch unbinds
Eolian magic from their lucid wombs:
Then old songs waken from encloudèd tombs;
Old ditties sigh above their father's grave;
Ghosts of melodious prophesyings rave
Round every spot where trod Apollo's foot;   790
Bronze clarions awake, and faintly bruit,
Where long ago a Giant Battle was;
And, from the turf, a lullaby doth pass
In every place where infant Orpheus slept.
Feel we these things?—that moment have we stept
Into a sort of oneness, and our state
Is like a floating spirit's. But there are
Richer entanglements, enthralments far
More self-destroying, leading, by degrees,
To the chief intensity: the crown of these   800
Is made of love and friendship, and sits high
Upon the forehead of humanity.
All its more ponderous and bulky worth
Is friendship, whence there ever issues forth
A steady splendour; but at the tip-top,
There hangs by unseen film, an orbèd drop
Of light, and that is love: its influence,
Thrown in our eyes, genders a novel sense,
At which we start and fret; till in the end,
Melting into its radiance, we blend,   810
Mingle, and so become a part of it,—
Nor with aught else can our souls interknit
So wingedly: when we combine therewith,
Life's self is nourished by its proper pith,
And we are nurtured like a pelican brood.
Aye, so delicious is the unsating food,

33

That men, who might have tower'd in the van
Of all the congregated world, to fan
And winnow from the coming step of time
All chaff of custom, wipe away all slime   820
Left by men-slugs and human serpentry,
Have been content to let occasion die,
Whilst they did sleep in love's elysium.
And, truly, I would rather be struck dumb,
Than speak against this ardent listlessness:
For I have ever thought that it might bless
The world with benefits unknowingly;
As does the nightingale, upperched high,
And cloister'd among cool and bunched leaves—
She sings but to her love, nor e'er conceives   830
How tiptoe Night holds back her dark-grey hood.
Just so may love, although 'tis understood
The mere commingling of passionate breath,
Produce more than our searching witnesseth:
What I know not: but who, of men, can tell
That flowers would bloom, or that green fruit would swell
To melting pulp, that fish would have bright mail,
The earth its dower of river, wood, and vale,
The meadows runnels, runnels pebble-stones,
The seed its harvest, or the lute its tones,   840
Tones ravishment, or ravishment its sweet,
If human souls did never kiss and greet?

To FANNY KEATS
Wednesday 10 Sept. [*1817*]
    . . . When I saw you last I told you of my intention of going to
Oxford and 'tis now a Week since I disembark'd from his Whip-
ship's Coach the Defiance in this place. I am living in Magdalen
Hall on a visit to a young Man with whom I have not been long
acquainted, but whom I like very much—we lead very industrious

lives he in general Studies and I in proceeding **at a** pretty good rate with a Poem which I hope you will see early in the next year— Perhaps you might like to know what I am writing about—I will tell you—

Many Years ago there was a young handsome Shepherd who fed his flocks on a Mountain's Side called Latmus—he was a very contemplative sort of a Person and lived solitry among the trees and Plains little thinking—that such a beautiful Creature as the Moon was growing mad in Love with him—However so it was; and when he was asleep on the Grass, she used to come down from heaven and admire him excessively from a long time; and at last could not refrain from car[r]ying him away in her arms to the top of that high Mountain Latmus while he was a dreaming—but I dare say [you] have read this and all the other beautiful Tales which have come down from the ancient times of that beautiful Greece. If you have not let me know and I will tell you more at large of others quite as delightful—

This Oxford I have no doubt is the finest City in the world—it is full of old Gothic buildings—Spires—towers—Quadrangles— Cloisters Groves &[c.] and is surrounded with more Clear streams than ever I saw together—I take a Walk by the Side of one of them every Evening and thank God, we have not had a drop of rain these many days. . . .

Lines rhymed in a Letter received

(by J. H. R.) from Oxford

I

THE Gothic looks solemn,
  The plain Doric column
Supports an old Bishop and Crosier;
  The mouldering arch,
  Shaded o'er by a larch
Stands next door to Wilson the Hosier.

II

Vice—that is, by turns,—
O'er pale visages mourns
The black tassell trencher or common hat;
The Chantry boy sings,
The Steeple-bell rings,
And as for the Chancellor—*dominat.*

10

There are plenty of trees,
And plenty of ease,
And plenty of fat deer for Parsons;
And when it is venison
Short is the benison,—
Then each on a leg or thigh fastens

To BENJAMIN BAILEY
[*Saturday 22 Nov. 1817*]

. . . I wish you knew all that I think about Genius and the Heart
—and yet I think you are thoroughly acquainted with my inner-
most breast in that respect or you could not have known me even
thus long and still hold me worthy to be your dear friend. In passing
however I must say of one thing that has pressed upon me lately
and encreased my Humility and capability of submission and that
is this truth—Men of Genius are great as certain ethereal Chemicals
operating on the Mass of neutral intellect—by [*for* but] they have
not any individuality, any determined Character. I would call the
top and head of those who have a proper self Men of Power—

But I am running my head into a Subject which I am certain I
could not do justice to under five years s[t]udy and 3 vols octavo—
and moreover long to be talking about the Imagination—so my
dear Bailey do not think of this unpleasant affair if possible—do
not—I defy any ha[r]m to come of it—I defy—I'll shall write to

Crips this Week and reque[s]t him to tell me all his goings on from time to time by Letter whererever I may be—it will all go on well —so don't because you have suddenly discover'd a Coldness in Haydon suffer yourself to be teased. Do not my dear fellow. O I wish I was as certain of the end of all your troubles as that of your momentary start about the authenticity of the Imagination. I am certain of nothing but of the holiness of the Heart's affections and the truth of Imagination—What the imagination seizes as Beauty must be truth—whether it existed before or not—for I have the same Idea of all our Passions as of Love they are all in their sublime, creative of essential Beauty—In a Word, you may know my favorite Speculation by my first Book and the little song I sent in my last —which is a representation from the fancy of the probable mode of operating in these Matters—The Imagination may be compared to Adam's dream—he awoke and found it truth. I am the more zealous in this affair, because I have never yet been able to perceive how any thing can be known for truth by consequitive reasoning—and yet it must be—Can it be that even the greatest Philosopher ever arrived at his goal without putting aside numerous objections—However it may be, O for a Life of Sensations rather than of Thoughts! It is 'a Vision in the form of Youth' a Shadow of reality to come— and this consideration has further conv[i]nced me for it has come as auxiliary to another favorite Speculation of mine, that we shall enjoy ourselves here after by having what we called happiness on Earth repeated in a finer tone and so repeated—And yet such a fate can only befall those who delight in sensation rather than hunger as you do after Truth—Adam's dream will do here and seems to be a conviction that Imagination and its empyreal reflection is the same as human Life and its spiritual repetition. But as I was saying —the simple imaginative Mind may have its rewards in the repeti[ti]on of its own silent Working coming continually on the spirit with a fine suddenness—to compare great things with small— have you never by being surprised with an old Melody—in a delicious place—by a delicious voice, fe[l]t over again your very speculations and surmises at the time it first operated on your soul

—do you not remember forming to yourself the singer's face more beautiful that [*for* than] it was possible and yet with the elevation of the Moment you did not think so—even then you were mounted on the Wings of Imagination so high—that the Prototype must be here after—that delicious face you will see—What a time! I am continually running away from the subject—sure this cannot be exactly the case with a complex Mind—one that is imaginative and at the same time careful of its fruits—who would exist partly on sensation partly on thought—to whom it is necessary that years should bring the philosophic Mind—such an one I consider your's and therefore it is necessary to your eternal Happiness that you not only drink of this old Wine of Heaven, which I shall call the redigestion of our most ethereal Musings on Earth; but also increase in knowledge and know all things. . . .

Extract from

Endymion

BOOK IV. LINES 512–548

There lies a den,
Beyond the seeming confines of the space
Made for the soul to wander in and trace
Its own existence, of remotest glooms.
Dark regions are around it, where the tombs
Of buried griefs the spirit sees, but scarce
One hour doth linger weeping, for the pierce
Of new-born woe it feels more inly smart:
And in these regions many a venom'd dart   520
At random flies; they are the proper home
Of every ill: the man is yet to come
Who hath not journeyed in this native hell.

But few have ever felt how calm and well
Sleep may be had in that deep den of all.
There anguish does not sting; nor pleasure pall:
Woe-hurricanes beat ever at the gate,
Yet all is still within and desolate.
Beset with painful gusts, within ye hear
No sound so loud as when on curtain'd bier   530
The death-watch tick is stifled. Enter none
Who strive therefore: on the sudden it is won.
Just when the sufferer begins to burn,
Then it is free to him; and from an urn,
Still fed by melting ice, he takes a draught—
Young Semele such richness never quaft
In her maternal longing! Happy gloom!
Dark Paradise! where pale becomes the bloom
Of health by due; where silence dreariest
Is most articulate; where hopes infest;   540
Where those eyes are the brightest far that keep
Their lids shut longest in a dreamless sleep.
O happy spirit-home! O wondrous soul!
Pregnant with such a den to save the whole
In thine own depth. Hail, gentle Carian!
For, never since thy griefs and woes began,
Hast thou felt so content: a grievous feud
Hath led thee to this Cave of Quietude.   548

Stanzas

I

In a drear-nighted December,
    Too happy, happy tree,
Thy branches ne'er remember
    Their green felicity:

39

The north cannot undo them,
With a sleety whistle through them;
Nor frozen thawings glue them
    From budding at the prime.

II

In a drear-nighted December,
    Too happy, happy brook,   10
Thy bubblings ne'er remember
    Apollo's summer look;
But with a sweet forgetting,
They stay their crystal fretting,
Never, never petting
    About the frozen time.

III

Ah! would 'twere so with many
    A gentle girl and boy!
But were there ever any
    Writh'd not at passed joy?   20
The feel of not to feel it,
When there is none to heal it,
Nor numbed sense to steal it,
    Was never said in rhyme.

To GEORGE AND THOMAS KEATS
[*Sunday 21 Dec. 1817*]
    ... Brown & Dilke walked with me & back from the Christmas
pantomime. I had not a dispute but a disquisition with Dilke, on
various subjects; several things dovetailed in my mind, & at once
it struck me, what quality went to form a Man of Achievement
especially in Literature & which Shakespeare possessed so enor-
mously—I mean *Negative Capability*, that is when man is capable

of being in uncertainties, Mysteries, doubts, without any irritable reaching after fact & reason—Coleridge, for instance, would let go by a fine isolated verisimilitude caught from the Penetralium of mystery, from being incapable of remaining content with half knowledge. This pursued through Volumes would perhaps take us no further than this, that with a great poet the sense of Beauty overcomes every other consideration, or rather obliterates all consideration. . . .

To Mrs. Reynolds's Cat

CAT! who hast past thy Grand Climacteric,
   How many mice and Rats hast in thy days
   Destroy'd?—how many tit bits stolen? Gaze
With those bright languid segments green and prick
Those velvet ears—but pr'ythee do not stick
   Thy latent talons in me—and upraise
   Thy gentle mew—and tell me all thy frays
Of Fish and Mice, and Rats and tender chick.
Nay look not down, nor lick thy dainty wrists—
   For all the weezy Asthma,—and for all   10
Thy tail's tip is nicked off—and though the fists
   Of many a Maid have given thee many a maul,
Still is that fur as soft as when the lists
   In youth thou enter'dst on glass-bottled wall.

On sitting down to read King Lear once again

O GOLDEN tongued Romance, with serene lute!
  Fair plumed Syren, Queen of far-away!
  Leave melodizing on this wintry day,
Shut up thine olden pages, and be mute:
Adieu! for, once again, the fierce dispute
  Betwixt damnation and impassion'd clay
  Must I burn through; once more humbly assay
The bitter-sweet of this Shakespearian fruit:
Chief Poet! and ye clouds of Albion,
  Begetters of our deep eternal theme!   10
When through the old oak Forest I am gone,
  Let me not wander in a barren dream,
But, when I am consumed in the fire
Give me new Phoenix wings to fly at my desire.

To GEORGE AND THOMAS KEATS
Friday, 23 January 1818
  . . . I left off short in my last, just as I began an account of a private
theatrical—Well it was of the lowest order, all greasy & oily,
insomuch that if they had lived in olden times, when signs were
hung over the doors; the only appropriate one for that oily place
would have been—a guttered Candle—They played John Bull The
Review. & it was to conclude with Bombastes Furioso—I saw
from a Box the 1st Act of John Bull, then I went to Drury & did
not return till it was over; when by Wells' interest we got behind
the scenes. There was not a yard wide all the way round for actors,
scene-shifters & interlopers to move in; for 'Nota Bene' the Green

Room was under the stage and there was I threatened over & over again to be turned out by the oily scene-shifters—there did I hear a little painted Trollop own, very candidly, that she had failed in Mary, with a "damned if she'd play a serious part again, as long as she lived", & at the same time she was habited as the Quaker in the Review—there was a quarrel & a fat good-natured looking girl in soldiers Clothes wished she had only been a man for Tom's sake— One fellow began a song, but an unlucky finger-point from the Gallery sent him off like a shot, One chap was dressed to kill for the King in Bombastes, & he stood at the edge of the scene in the very sweat of anxiety to show himself, but Alas the thing was not played. the sweetest morsel of the night moreover was, that the musicians began pegging and fagging away at an overture—never did you see faces more in earnest, three times did they play it over, dropping all kinds of correctness & still did not the curtain draw up —Well then they went into a country-dance then into a region they well knew, into their old boonsome Pothouse, & then to see how pompous o' the sudden they turned; how they looked about & chatted; how they did not care a Damn; was a great treat. . . .

When I have fears

WHEN I have fears that I may cease to be
    Before my pen has glean'd my teeming brain,
Before high-piled books, in charact'ry,
    Hold like rich garners the full-ripen'd grain;
When I behold, upon the night's starr'd face,
    Huge cloudy symbols of a high romance,
And think that I may never live to trace
    Their shadows, with the magic hand of chance;
And when I feel, fair creature of an hour!

43

That I shall never look upon thee more, 10
Never have relish in the faery power
  Of unreflecting love!—then on the shore
Of the wide world I stand alone, and think
Till love and fame to nothingness do sink.

Lines on the Mermaid Tavern

SOULS of Poets dead and gone,
What Elysium have ye known,
Happy field or mossy cavern,
Choicer than the Mermaid Tavern?
Have ye tippled drink more fine
Than mine host's Canary wine?
Or are fruits of Paradise
Sweeter than those dainty pies
Of venison? O generous food!
Drest as though bold Robin Hood 10
Would, with his maid Marian,
Sup and bowse from horn and can.

  I have heard that on a day
Mine host's sign-board flew away,
Nobody knew whither, till
An astrologer's old quill
To a sheepskin gave the story,
Said he saw you in your glory,
Underneath a new-old sign
Sipping beverage divine, 20
And pledging with contented smack
The Mermaid in the Zodiac.

Souls of Poets dead and gone,
What Elysium have ye known,
Happy field or mossy cavern,
Choicer than the Mermaid Tavern?

To JOHN HAMILTON REYNOLDS
[*Thursday 19 Feb. 1818*]
My dear Reynolds,

I have an idea that a Man might pass a very pleasant life in this manner—let him on any certain day read a certain page of full Poesy or distilled Prose and let him wander with it, and muse upon it, and reflect from it, and bring home to it, and prophesy upon it, and dream upon it—untill it becomes stale—but when will it do so? Never—When Man has arrived at a certain ripeness in intellect any one grand and spiritual passage serves him as a starting post towards all "the two-and thirty Pallaces" How happy is such a "voyage of conception,' what delicious diligent Indolence! A doze upon a Sofa does not hinder it, and a nap upon Clover engenders ethereal finger-pointings—the prattle of a child gives it wings, and the converse of middle age a strength to beat them—a strain of musick conducts to 'an odd angle of the Isle' and when the leaves whisper it puts a 'girdle round the earth. Nor will this sparing touch of noble Books be any irreverance to their Writers—for perhaps the honors paid by Man to Man are trifles in comparison to the Benefit done by great Works to the 'Spirit and pulse of good' by their mere passive existence. Memory should not be called knowledge—Many have original Minds who do not think it—they are led away by Custom—Now it appears to me that almost any Man may like the Spider spin from his own inwards his own airy Citadel—the points of leaves and twigs on which the Spider begins her work are few and she fills the Air with a beautiful circuiting: man should be content with as few points to tip with the fine Webb of his Soul and wave a tapestry empyrean—full of Symbols for his spiritual eye, of softness for his spiritual touch, of space for his

45

wandering of distinctness for his Luxury—But the Minds of Mortals are so different and bent on such diverse Journeys that it may at first appear impossible for any common taste and fellowship to exist between two or three under these suppositions—It is however quite the contrary—Minds would leave each other in contrary directions, traverse each other in Numberless points, and all [for at] last greet each other at the Journeys end—A old Man and a child would talk together and the old Man be led on his Path, and the child left thinking—Man should not dispute or assert but whisper results to his neighbour, and thus by every germ of Spirit sucking the Sap from mould ethereal every human being might become great, and Humanity instead of being a wide heath of Furse and Briars with here and there a remote Oak or Pine, would become a grand democracy of Forest Trees. . . .

To JOHN TAYLOR
[*Friday*] *27 February 1818*
 . . . In Poetry I have a few Axioms, and you will see how far I am from their Centre. 1st I think Poetry should surprise by a fine excess and not by Singularity—it should strike the Reader as a wording of his own highest thoughts, and appear almost a Remembrance—2nd Its touches of Beauty should never be half way ther[e]by making the reader breathless instead of content: the rise, the progress, the setting of imagery should like the Sun come natural natural too him—shine over him and set soberly although in magnificence leaving him in the Luxury of twilight—but it is easier to think what Poetry should be than to write it—and this leads me on to another axiom. That if Poetry comes not as naturally as the Leaves to a tree it had better not come at all. . . .

Extract from

Isabella; or The Pot of Basil

XIV

With her two brothers this fair lady dwelt,   105
  Enriched from ancestral merchandize,
And for them many a weary hand did swelt
  In torched mines and noisy factories,
And many once proud-quiver'd loins did melt
  In blood from stinging whip;—with hollow eyes   110
Many all day in dazzling river stood,
To take the rich-ored driftings of the flood.

XV

For them the Ceylon diver held his breath,
  And went all naked to the hungry shark;
For them his ears gush'd blood; for them in death
  The seal on the cold ice with piteous bark
Lay full of darts; for them alone did seethe
  A thousand men in troubles wide and dark:
Half-ignorant they turn'd an easy wheel,
That set sharp racks at work, to pinch and peel.   120

XVI

Why were they proud? Because their marble founts
  Gush'd with more pride than do a wretch's tears?—
Why were they proud? Because fair orange-mounts
  Were of more soft ascent than lazar stairs?—
Why were they proud? Because red-lin'd accounts
  Were richer than the songs of Grecian years?—
Why were they proud? again we ask aloud,
Why in the name of Glory were they proud?

47

XVII

Yet were these Florentines as self-retired
   In hungry pride and gainful cowardice,   130
As two close Hebrews in that land inspired,
   Paled in and vineyarded from beggar-spies;
The hawks of ship-mast forests—the untired
   And pannier'd mules for ducats and old lies—
Quick cat's-paws on the generous stray-away,—
Great wits in Spanish, Tuscan, and Malay.

XVIII

How was it these same ledger-men could spy
   Fair Isabella in her downy nest?
How could they find out in Lorenzo's eye
   A straying from his toil? Hot Egypt's pest   140
Into their vision covetous and sly!
How could these money-bags see east and west?—
Yet so they did—and every dealer fair
Must see behind, as doth the hunted hare.

XIX

O eloquent and famed Boccaccio!
   Of thee we now should ask forgiving boon,
And of thy spicy myrtles as they blow,
   And of thy roses amorous of the moon,
And of thy lilies, that do paler grow
   Now they can no more hear thy ghittern's tune,   150
For venturing syllables that ill beseem
The quiet glooms of such a piteous theme.

XX

Grant thou a pardon here, and then the tale
   Shall move on soberly, as it is meet;
There is no other crime, no mad assail
   To make old prose in modern rhyme more sweet:

But it is done—succeed the verse or fail—
    To honour thee, and thy gone spirit greet;
To stead thee as a verse in English tongue,
An echo of thee in the north-wind sung.   160

XXI

These brethren having found by many signs
    What love Lorenzo for their sister had,
And how she lov'd him too, each unconfines
    His bitter thoughts to other, well nigh mad
That he, the servant of their trade designs,
    Should in their sister's love be blithe and glad,
When 'twas their plan to coax her by degrees
To some high noble and his olive-trees.

XXII

And many a jealous conference had they,
    And many times they bit their lips alone,   170
Before they fix'd upon a surest way
    To make the youngster for his crime atone;
And at the last, these men of cruel clay
    Cut Mercy with a sharp knife to the bone;
For they resolved in some forest dim
To kill Lorenzo, and there bury him.

XXIII

So on a pleasant morning, as he leant
    Into the sun-rise, o'er the balustrade
Of the garden-terrace, towards him they bent
    Their footing through the dews; and to him said,   180
'You seem there in the quiet of content,
    'Lorenzo, and we are most loth to invade
'Calm speculation; but if you are wise,
'Bestride your steed while cold is in the skies.

49

XXIV

'To-day we purpose, aye, this hour we mount
  'To spur three leagues towards the Apennine;
'Come down, we pray thee, ere the hot sun count
  'His dewy rosary on the eglantine.'
Lorenzo, courteously as he was wont,
  Bow'd a fair greeting to these serpents' whine;   190
And went in haste, to get in readiness,
With belt, and spur, and bracing huntsman's dress.

And as he to the court-yard pass'd alone,
  Each third step did he pause, and listen'd oft
If he could hear his lady's matin-song,
  Or the light whisper of her footstep soft;
And as he thus over his passion hung,
  He heard a laugh full musical aloft;
When, looking up, he saw her features bright
Smile through an in-door lattice, all delight.   200

XXVI

'Love, Isabel!' said he, 'I was in pain
  'Lest I should miss to bid thee a good morrow:
'Ah! what if I should lose thee, when so fain
  'I am to stifle all the heavy sorrow
'Of a poor three hours' absence? but we'll gain
  'Out of the amorous dark what day doth borrow.
'Good bye! I'll soon be back.'—'Good bye!' said she:—
And as he went she chanted merrily.

So the two brothers and their murder'd man
  Rode past fair Florence, to where Arno's stream   210
Gurgles through straiten'd banks, and still doth fan
  Itself with dancing bulrush, and the bream

Keeps head against the freshets. Sick and wan
  The brothers' faces in the ford did seem,
Lorenzo's flush with love.—They pass'd the water
Into a forest quiet for the slaughter.

XXVIII

There was Lorenzo slain and buried in,
  There in that forest did his great love cease;
Ah! when a soul doth thus its freedom win,
  It aches in loneliness—is ill at peace   220
As the break-covert blood-hounds of such sin:
  They dipp'd their swords in the water, and did tease
Their horses homeward, with convulsed spur,
Each richer by his being a murderer.

To JOHN HAMILTON REYNOLDS
Sunday 3 May 1818

  . . . I will return to Wordsworth—whether or no he has an ex-
tended vision or a circumscribed grandeur—whether he is an eagle in
his nest, or on the wing—And to be more explicit and to show you
how tall I stand by the giant, I will put down a simile of human
life as far as I now perceive it; that is, to the point to which I say
we both have arrived at—Well—I compare human life to a large
Mansion of Many Apartments, two of which I can only describe,
the doors of the rest being as yet shut upon me—The first we step
into we call the infant or thoughtless Chamber, in which we remain
as long as we do not think—We remain there a long while, and
notwithstanding the doors of the second Chamber remain wide
open, showing a bright appearance, we care not to hasten to it; but
are at length imperceptibly impelled by the awakening of the think-
ing principle—within us—we no sooner get into the second
Chamber, which I shall call the Chamber of Maiden-Thought, than
we become intoxicated with the light and the atmosphere, we see

nothing but pleasant wonders, and think of delaying there for ever in delight: However among the effects this breathing is father of is that tremendous one of sharpening one's vision into the heart and nature of Man—of convincing one's nerves that the World is full of Misery and Heartbreak, Pain, Sickness and oppression—whereby This Chamber of Maiden Thought becomes gradually darken'd and at the same time on all sides of it many doors are set open—but all dark—all leading to dark passages—We see not the ballance of good and evil. We are in a Mist—*We* are now in that state—We feel the "burden of the Mystery," To this Point was Wordsworth come, as far as I can conceive when he wrote 'Tintern Abbey' and it seems to me that his Genius is explorative of those dark Passages. Now if we live, and go on thinking, we too shall explore them—he is a Genius and superior [to] us, in so far as he can, more than we, make discoveries, and shed a light in them—Here I must think Wordsworth is deeper than Milton—though I think it has depended more upon the general and gregarious advance of intellect, than individual greatness of Mind—From the Paradise Lost and the other Works of Milton, I hope it is not too presuming, even between ourselves to say, his Philosophy, human and divine, may be tolerably understood by one not much advanced in years, In his time englishmen were just emancipated from a great superstition—and Men had got hold of certain points and resting places in reasoning which were too newly born to be doubted, and too much opposed by the Mass of Europe not to be thought etherial and authentically divine—who could gainsay his ideas on virtue, vice, and Chastity in Comus, just at the time of the dismissal of Cod-pieces and a hundred other disgraces? who would not rest satisfied with his hintings at good and evil in the Paradise Lost, when just free from the inquisition and burrning in Smithfield? The Reformation produced such immediate and great benefits, that Protestantism was considered under the immediate eye of heaven, and its own remaining Dogmas and superstitions, then, as it were, regenerated, constituted those resting places and seeming sure points of Reasoning—from that I have mentioned, Milton, whatever he may have thought in the sequel, appears to have been content with these by his writings—He did not think into the human heart, as Wordsworth has done—Yet Milton as a Philosop[h]er, had sure as great powers as Wordsworth —What is then to be inferr'd? O many things—It proves there is really a grand march of intellect—, It proves that a mighty providence subdues the mightiest Minds to the service of the time being, whether it be in human Knowledge or Religion. . . .

To THOMAS KEATS
Saturday 27 June 1818

. . . We arose this morning at six, because we call it a day of rest, having to call on Wordsworth who lives only two miles hence—before breakfast we went to see the Ambleside water fall. The morning beautiful—the walk easy among the hills. We, I may say, fortunately, missed the direct path, and after wandering a little found it out by the noise—for, mark you, it is buried in trees, in the bottom of the valley—the stream itself is interesting throughout with "mazy error over pendant shades." Milton meant a smooth river—this is buffetting all the way on a rocky bed ever various— but the waterfall itself, which I came suddenly upon, gave me a pleasant twinge. First we stood a little below the head about half way down the first fall, buried deep in trees, and saw it streaming down two more descents to the depth of near fifty feet—then we went on a jut of rock nearly level with the second fall-head, where the first fall was above us, and the third below our feet still—at the same time we saw that the water was divided by a sort of cataract island on whose other side burst out a glorious stream—then the thunder and the freshness. At the same time the different falls have as different characters; the first darting down the slate-rock like an arrow; the second spreading out like a fan—the third dashed into a mist—and the one on the other side of the rock a sort of mixture of all these. We afterwards moved away a space, and saw nearly the whole more mild, streaming silverly through the trees. What astonishes me more than any thing is the tone, the coloring, the slate, the stone, the moss, the rock-weed; or, if I may so say, the intellect, the countenance of such places. The space, the magnitude of mountains and waterfalls are well imagined before one sees them; but this countenance or intellectual tone must surpass every imagination and defy any remembrance. I shall learn poetry here and shall henceforth write more than ever, for the abstract endeavor of being able to add a mite to that mass of beauty which is harvested from these grand materials, by the finest spirits, and put into etherial existence for the relish of one's fellows. I cannot think with Hazlitt that these scenes make man appear little. I never forgot my stature so completely—I live in the eye; and my imagination, surpassed, is at rest. . . .

Old Meg

OLD MEG she was a Gipsey,
  And liv'd upon the Moors;
Her bed it was the brown heath turf,
  And her house was out of doors.

Her apples were swart blackberries,
  Her currants, pods o' broom;
Her wine was dew of the wild white rose,
  Her book a churchyard tomb.

Her Brothers were the craggy hills,
  Her Sisters larchen trees;   10
Alone with her great family
  She liv'd as she did please.

No breakfast had she many a morn,
    No dinner many a noon,
And, 'stead of supper, she would stare
    Full hard against the Moon.

But every morn, of woodbine fresh
    She made her garlanding,
And, every night, the dark glen Yew
    She wove, and she would sing.   20

And with her fingers, old and brown,
    She plaited Mats o' Rushes,
And gave them to the Cottagers
    She met among the Bushes.

Old Meg was brave as Margaret Queen
    And tall as Amazon;
An old red blanket cloak she wore,
    A chip hat had she on.
God rest her aged bones somewhere!
    She died full long agone!   30

Lines written in the Highlands after a Visit to Burns's Country

THERE is a charm in footing slow across a silent plain,
Where patriot battle has been fought, when glory had the gain;
There is a pleasure on the heath where Druids old have been,
Where mantles grey have rustled by and swept the nettles green;
There is a joy in every spot made known by times of old,
New to the feet, although each tale a hundred times be told;

There is a deeper joy than all, more solemn in the heart,
More parching to the tongue than all, of more divine a smart,
When weary steps forget themselves upon a pleasant turf,
Upon hot sand, or flinty road, or sea-shore iron scurf,   10
Toward the castle or the cot, where long ago was born
One who was great through mortal days, and died of fame unshorn:
Light heather-bells may tremble then, but they are far away;
Wood-lark may sing from sandy fern,—the Sun may hear his lay;
Runnels may kiss the grass on shelves and shallows clear,
But their low voices are not heard, though come on travels drear;
Blood-red the Sun may set behind black mountain peaks;
Blue tides may sluice and drench their time in caves and weedy
    creeks;
Eagles may seem to sleep wing-wide upon the air;
Ring-doves may fly convuls'd across to some high-cedar'd lair;
But the forgotten eye is still fast lidded to the ground,   21
As Palmer's, that with weariness, mid-desert shrine hath found.
At such a time the soul's a child, in childhood is the brain;
Forgotten is the worldly heart—alone, it beats in vain.—
Aye, if a madman could have leave to pass a healthful day
To tell his forehead's swoon and faint when first began decay,
He might make tremble many a one whose spirit had gone forth
To find a Bard's low cradle-place about the silent North!
Scanty the hour and few the steps beyond the bourn of care,
Beyond the sweet and bitter world,—beyond it unaware!   30
Scanty the hour and few the steps, because a longer stay
Would bar return, and make a man forget his mortal way:
O horrible! to lose the sight of well-remember'd face,
Of Brother's eyes, of Sister's brow—constant to every place;
Filling the air, as on we move, with portraiture intense;
More warm than those heroic tints that pain a painter's sense,
When shapes of old come striding by, and visages of old,
Locks shining black, hair scanty grey, and passions manifold.
No, no, that horror cannot be, for at the cable's length
Man feels the gentle anchor pull and gladdens in its strength:—

One hour, half-idiot, he stands by mossy waterfall,
But in the very next he reads his soul's memorial:—
He reads it on the mountain's height, where chance he may sit down
Upon rough marble diadem—that hill's eternal crown.
Yet be his anchor e'er so fast, room is there for a prayer
That man may never lose his mind on mountains black and bare;
That he may stray league after league some great birthplace to find
And keep his vision clear from speck, his inward sight unblind.

To THOMAS KEATS
Sunday 26 July 1818
. . . I am puzzled how to give you an Idea of Staffa. It can only
be represented by a first rate drawing—One may compare the sur-
face of the Island to a roof—this roof is supported by grand pillars
of basalt standing together as thick as honey combs. The finest thing
is Fingal's Cave—it is entirely a hollowing out of Basalt Pillars.
Suppose now the Giants who rebelled against Jove had taken a
whole Mass of black columns and bound them together like bunches
of matches—and then with immense Axes had made a cavern in
the body of these columns—of course the roof and floor must be
composed of the broken ends of the Columns—such is fingal's Cave
except that the Sea has done the work of excavations and is con-
tinually dashing there—so that we walk along the sides of the cave
on the pillars which are left as if for convenient Stairs—the roof is
arched somewhat gothic wise and the length of some of the entire
side pillars is 50 feet—About the island you might seat an army of
Men each on a pillar—The length of the Cave is 120 feet and from
its extremity the view into the sea through the large Arch at the
entrance—the colour of the colums is a sort of black with a lurking
gloom of purple therin—For solemnity and grandeur it far surpasses
the finest Cathedrall—At the extremity of the Cave there is a small
perforation into another cave, at which the waters meeting and
buffetting each other there is sometimes produced a report as of a

cannon heard as far as Iona which must be 12 Miles—As we approached in the boat there was such a fine swell of the sea that the pillars appeared rising immediately out of the crystal—But it is impossible to describe it— ...

Hyperion

A Fragment

BOOK I

DEEP in the shady sadness of a vale
Far sunken from the healthy breath of morn,
Far from the fiery noon, and eve's one star,
Sat gray-hair'd Saturn, quiet as a stone,
Still as the silence round about his lair;
Forest on forest hung above his head
Like cloud on cloud. No stir of air was there,
Not so much life as on a summer's day
Robs not one light seed from the feather'd grass,
But where the dead leaf fell, there did it rest.   10
A stream went voiceless by, still deadened more
By reason of his fallen divinity
Spreading a shade: the naiad 'mid her reeds
Press'd her cold finger closer to her lips.

Along the margin-sand large foot-marks went,
No further than to where his feet had stray'd,
And slept there since. Upon the sodden ground
His old right hand lay nerveless, listless, dead,
Unsceptred; and his realmless eyes were closed;

While his bow'd head seem'd list'ning to the Earth,   20
His ancient mother, for some comfort yet.

  It seem'd no force could wake him from his place;
But there came one, who with a kindred hand
Touch'd his wide shoulders, after bending low
With reverence, though to one who knew it not.
She was a Goddess of the infant world;
By her in stature the tall Amazon
Had stood a pigmy's height: she would have ta'en
Achilles by the hair and bent his neck;
Or with a finger stay'd Ixion's wheel.   30
Her face was large as that of Memphian sphinx,
Pedestal'd haply in a palace court,
When sages look'd to Egypt for their lore.
But oh! how unlike marble was that face:
How beautiful, if sorrow had not made
Sorrow more beautiful than Beauty's self.
There was a listening fear in her regard,
As if calamity had but begun;
As if the vanward clouds of evil days
Had spent their malice, and the sullen rear   40
Was with its stored thunder labouring up.
One hand she press'd upon that aching spot
Where beats the human heart, as if just there,
Though an immortal, she felt cruel pain:
The other upon Saturn's bended neck
She laid, and to the level of his ear
Leaning with parted lips, some words she spake
In solemn tenour and deep organ tone:
Some mourning words, which in our feeble tongue
Would come in these like accents; O how frail   50
To that large utterance of the early Gods!
'Saturn, look up!—though wherefore, poor old King?
'I have no comfort for thee, no not one:

'I cannot say, "O wherefore sleepest thou?"
'For heaven is parted from thee, and the earth
'Knows thee not, thus afflicted, for a God;
'And ocean too, with all its solemn noise,
'Has from thy sceptre pass'd; and all the air
'Is emptied of thine hoary majesty.
'Thy thunder, conscious of the new command,   60
'Rumbles reluctant o'er our fallen house;
'And thy sharp lightning in unpractised hands
'Scorches and burns our once serene domain.
'O aching time! O moments big as years!
'All as ye pass swell out the monstrous truth,
'And press it so upon our weary griefs
'That unbelief has not a space to breathe.
'Saturn, sleep on:—O thoughtless, why did I
'Thus violate thy slumbrous solitude?
'Why should I ope thy melancholy eyes?   70
'Saturn, sleep on! while at thy feet I weep.'

   As when, upon a tranced summer-night,
Those green-rob'd senators of mighty woods,
Tall oaks, branch-charmed by the earnest stars,
Dream, and so dream all night without a stir,
Save from one gradual solitary gust
Which comes upon the silence, and dies off,
As if the ebbing air had but one wave;
So came these words and went; the while in tears
She touch'd her fair large forehead to the ground,   80
Just where her fallen hair might be outspread
A soft and silken mat for Saturn's feet.
One moon, with alteration slow, had shed
Her silver seasons four upon the night,
And still these two were postured motionless,
Like natural sculpture in cathedral cavern;
The frozen God still couchant on the earth,

And the sad Goddess weeping at his feet:
Until at length old Saturn lifted up
His faded eyes, and saw his kingdom gone,   90
And all the gloom and sorrow of the place,
And that fair kneeling Goddess; and then spake,
As with a palsied tongue, and while his beard
Shook horrid with such aspen-malady:
'O tender spouse of gold Hyperion,
'Thea, I feel thee ere I see thy face;
'Look up, and let me see our doom in it;
'Look up, and tell me if this feeble shape
'Is Saturn's; tell me, if thou hear'st the voice
'Of Saturn; tell me, if this wrinkling brow,   100
'Naked and bare of its great diadem,
'Peers like the front of Saturn. Who had power
'To make me desolate? whence came the strength?
'How was it nurtur'd to such bursting forth,
'While Fate seem'd strangled in my nervous grasp?
'But it is so; and I am smother'd up,
'And buried from all godlike exercise
'Of influence benign on planets pale,
'Of admonitions to the winds and seas,
'Of peaceful sway above man's harvesting,   110
'And all those acts which Deity supreme
'Doth ease its heart of love in.—I am gone
'Away from my own bosom: I have left
'My strong identity, my real self,
'Somewhere between the throne, and where I sit
'Here on this spot of earth. Search, Thea, search!
'Open thine eyes eterne, and sphere them round
'Upon all space: space starr'd, and lorn of light;
'Space region'd with life-air; and barren void;
'Spaces of fire, and all the yawn of hell.—   120
'Search, Thea, search! and tell me, if thou seest
'A certain shape or shadow, making way

61

'With wings or chariot fierce to repossess
'A heaven he lost erewhile: it must—it must
'Be of ripe progress—Saturn must be King.
'Yes, there must be a golden victory;
'There must be Gods thrown down, and trumpets blown
'Of triumph calm, and hymns of festival
'Upon the gold clouds metropolitan,
'Voices of soft proclaim, and silver stir   130
'Of strings in hollow shells; and there shall be
'Beautiful things made new, for the surprise
'Of the sky-children; I will give command:
'Thea! Thea! Thea! where is Saturn?'

    This passion lifted him upon his feet,
And made his hands to struggle in the air,
His Druid locks to shake and ooze with sweat,
His eyes to fever out, his voice to cease.
He stood, and heard not Thea's sobbing deep;
A little time, and then again he snatch'd   140
Utterance thus.—'But cannot I create?
'Cannot I form? Cannot I fashion forth
'Another world, another universe,
'To overbear and crumble this to nought?
'Where is another Chaos? Where?'—That word
Found way unto Olympus, and made quake
The rebel three.—Thea was startled up,
And in her bearing was a sort of hope,
As thus she quick-voic'd spake, yet full of awe.
    'This cheers our fallen house: come to our friends,   150
'O Saturn! come away, and give them heart;
'I know the covert, for thence came I hither.'
Thus brief; then with beseeching eyes she went
With backward footing through the shade a space:
He follow'd, and she turn'd to lead the way

Through aged boughs, that yielded like the mist
Which eagles cleave upmounting from their nest.

Meanwhile in other realms big tears were shed,
More sorrow like to this, and such like woe,
Too huge for mortal tongue or pen of scribe: 160
The Titans fierce, self-hid or prison-bound,
Groan'd for the old allegiance once more,
And listen'd in sharp pain for Saturn's voice.
But one of the whole mammoth-brood still kept
His sov'reignty, and rule, and majesty;—
Blazing Hyperion on his orbed fire
Still sat, still snuff'd the incense, teeming up
From Man to the sun's God; yet unsecure:
For as among us mortals omens drear
Fright and perplex, so also shuddered he—   170
Not at dog's howl, or gloom-bird's hated screech,
Or the familiar visiting of one
Upon the first toll of his passing-bell,
Or prophesyings of the midnight lamp;
But horrors, portion'd to a giant nerve,
Oft made Hyperion ache. His palace bright
Bastion'd with pyramids of glowing gold,
And touched with shade of bronzed obelisks,
Glar'd a blood-red through all its thousand courts,
Arches, and domes, and fiery galleries;   180
And all its curtains of Aurorian clouds
Flush'd angerly: while sometimes eagle's wings,
Unseen before by Gods or wondering men,
Darken'd the place; and neighing steeds were heard,
Not heard before by Gods or wondering men.
Also, when he would taste the spicy wreaths
Of incense, breath'd aloft from sacred hills,
Instead of sweets, his ample palate took
Savour of poisonous brass and metal sick:

63

And so, when harbour'd in the sleepy west,
After the full completion of fair day,—
For rest divine upon exalted couch
And slumber in the arms of melody,
He pac'd away the pleasant hours of ease
With stride colossal, on from hall to hall;
While far within each aisle and deep recess,
His winged minions in close clusters stood,
Amaz'd and full of fear; like anxious men
Who on wide plains gather in panting troops,
When earthquakes jar their battlements and towers.   200
Even now, while Saturn, rous'd from icy trance,
Went step for step with Thea through the woods,
Hyperion, leaving twilight in the rear,
Came slope upon the threshold of the west;
Then, as he was wont, his palace-door flew ope
In smoothest silence, save what solemn tubes,
Blown by the serious Zephyrs, gave of sweet
And wandering sounds, slow-breathed melodies;
And like a rose in vermeil tint and shape,
In fragrance soft, and coolness to the eye,   210
That inlet to severe magnificence
Stood full blown, for the God to enter in.

He enter'd, but he enter'd full of wrath
His flaming robes stream'd out beyond his heels,
And gave a roar, as if of earthly fire,
That scar'd away the meek ethereal Hours
And made their dove-wings tremble. On he flared,
From stately nave to nave, from vault to vault,
Through bowers of fragrant and enwreathed light,
And diamond-paved lustrous long arcades,   220
Until he reach'd the great main cupola;
There standing fierce beneath, he stampt his foot,
And from the basements deep to the high towers

Jarr'd his own golden region; and before
The quavering thunder thereupon had ceas'd,
His voice leapt out, despite of godlike curb,
To this result: 'O dreams of day and night!
'O monstrous forms! O effigies of pain!
'O spectres busy in a cold, cold gloom!
'O lank-eared Phantoms of black-weeded Pools!   230
'Why do I know ye? why have I seen ye? why
'Is my eternal essence thus distraught
'To see and to behold these horrors new?
'Saturn is fallen, am I too to fall?
'Am I to leave this haven of my rest,
'This cradle of my glory, this soft clime,
'This calm luxuriance of blissful light,
'These crystalline pavilions, and pure fanes,
'Of all my lucent empire? It is left
'Deserted, void, nor any haunt of mine.   240
'The blaze, the splendor, and the symmetry
'I cannot see—but darkness, death and darkness.
'Even here, into my centre of repose,
'The shady visions come to domineer,
'Insult, and blind, and stifle my pomp.—
'Fall!—No, by Tellus and her briny robes!
'Over the fiery frontier of my realms
'I will advance a terrible right arm
'Shall scare that infant Thunderer, rebel Jove,
'And bid old Saturn take his throne again.'—   250
He spake, and ceas'd, the while a heavier threat
Held struggle with his throat but came not forth;
For as in theatres of crowded men
Hubbub increases more they call out 'Hush!'
So at Hyperion's words the Phantoms pale
Bestirr'd themselves, thrice horrible and cold;
And from the mirror'd level where he stood
A mist arose, as from a scummy marsh.

At this, through all his bulk an agony
Crept gradual, from the feet unto the crown,   260
Like a lithe serpent vast and muscular
Making slow way, with head and neck convuls'd
From over-strained might. Releas'd, he fled
To the eastern gates, and full six dewy hours
Before the dawn in season due should blush,
He breath'd fierce breath against the sleepy portals,
Clear'd them of heavy vapours, burst them wide
Suddenly on the ocean's chilly streams.
The planet orb of fire, whereon he rode
Each day from east to west the heavens through,   270
Spun round in sable curtaining of clouds;
Not therefore veiled quite, blindfold, and hid,
But ever and anon the glancing spheres,
Circles, and arcs, and broad-belting colure,
Glow'd through, and wrought upon the muffling dark
Sweet-shaped lightnings from the nadir deep
Up to the zenith,—heiroglyphics old,
Which sages and keen-eyed astologers
Then living on the earth, with labouring thought
Won from the gaze of many centuries: 280
Now lost, save what we find on remnants huge
Of stone, or marble swart; their import gone,
Their wisdom long since fled.—Two wings this orb
Possess'd for glory, two fair argent wings,
Ever exalted at the God's approach
And now, from forth the gloom their plumes immense
Rose, one by one, till all outspreaded were;
While still the dazzling globe maintain'd eclipse,
Awaiting for Hyperion's command.
Fain would he have commanded, fain took throne   290
And bid the day begin, if but for change.
He might not:—No, though a primeval God:
The sacred seasons might not be disturb'd.

Therefore the operations of the dawn
Stay'd in their birth, even as here 'tis told.
Those silver wings expanded sisterly,
Eager to sail their orb; the porches wide
Open'd upon the dusk demesnes of night
And the bright Titan, phrenzied with new woes,
Unus'd to bend, by hard compulsion bent   300
His spirit to the sorrow of the time;
And all along a dismal rack of clouds,
Upon the boundaries of day and night,
He stretch'd himself in grief and radiance faint.
There as he lay, the Heaven with its stars
Look'd down on him with pity, and the voice
Of Coelus, from the universal space,
Thus whisper'd low and solemn in his ear.
'O brightest of my children dear, earth-born
'And sky-engendered, Son of Mysteries   310
'All unrevealed even to the powers
'Which met at thy creating; at whose joys
'And palpitations sweet, and pleasures soft,
'I, Coelus, wonder, how they came and whence;
'And at the fruits thereof what shapes they be,
'Distinct and visible; symbols divine,
'Manifestations of that beauteous life
'Diffus'd unseen throughout eternal space:
'Of these new-form'd art thou, oh brightest child!
'Of these, thy brethren and the Goddesses!   320
'There is sad feud among ye, and rebellion
'Of son against his sire. I saw him fall,
'I saw my first-born tumbled from his throne!
'To me his arms were spread, to me his voice
'Found way from forth the thunders round his head!
'Pale was I, and in vapours hid my face.
'Art thou, too, near such doom? vague fear there is:
'For I have seen my sons must unlike Gods.

'Divine ye were created, and divine
'In sad demeanour, solemn, undisturb'd,   330
'Unruffled, like high Gods, ye liv'd and ruled:
'Now I behold in you fear, hope, and wrath;
'Actions of rage and passion; even as
'I see them, on the mortal world beneath,
'In men who die.—This is the grief, O Son!
'Sad sign of ruin, sudden dismay, and fall!
'Yet do thou strive; as thou art capable,
'As thou canst move about, an evident God;
'And canst oppose to each malignant hour
'Ethereal presence:—I am but a voice;   340
'My life is but the life of winds and tides,
'No more than winds and tides can I avail:—
'But thou canst.—Be thou therefore in the van
'Of Circumstance; yea, seize the arrow's barb
'Before the tense string murmur.—To the earth!
'For there thou wilt find Saturn, and his woes.
'Meantime I will keep watch on thy bright sun,
'And of thy seasons be a careful nurse.'—
Ere half this region-whisper had come down,
Hyperion arose, and on the stars   350
Lifted his curved lids, and kept them wide
Until it ceas'd; and still he kept them wide:
And still they were the same bright, patient stars
Then with a slow incline of his broad breast,
Like to a diver in the pearly seas,
Forward he stoop'd over the airy shore,
And plung'd all noiseless into the deep night.

BOOK II

JUST at the self-same beat of Time's wide wings
Hyperion slid into the rustled air,
And Saturn gain'd with Thea that sad place
Where Cybele and the bruised Titans mourn'd.

It was a den where no insulting light
Could glimmer on their tears; where their own groans
They felt, but heard not, for the solid roar
Of thunderous waterfalls and torrents hoarse,
Pouring a constant bulk, uncertain where.
Crag jutting forth to crag, and rocks that seem'd   10
Ever as if just rising from a sleep,
Forehead to forehead held their monstrous horns;
And thus in thousand hugest phantasies
Made a fit roofing to this nest of woe.
Instead of thrones, hard flint they sat upon,
Couches of rugged stone, and slaty ridge
Stubborn'd with iron. All were not assembled:
Some chain'd in torture, and some wandering.
Coeus, and Gyges, and Briareüs,
Typhon, and Dolor, and Porphyrion,   20
With many more, the brawniest in assault,
Were pent in regions of laborious breath;
Dungeon'd in opaque element, to keep
Their clenched teeth still clench'd, and all their limbs
Lock'd up like veins of metal, crampt and screw'd;
Without a motion, save of their big hearts
Heaving in pain, and horribly convuls'd
With sanguine feverous boiling gurge of pulse.
Mnemosyne was straying in the world;
Far from her moon had Phoebe wandered;   30
And many else were free to roam abroad,
But for the main, here found they covert drear.
Scarce images of life, one here, one there,
Lay vast and edgeways; like a dismal cirque
Of Druid stones, upon a forlorn moor,
When the chill rain begins at shut of eve,
In dull November, and their chancel vault,
The Heaven itself, is blinded throughout night.
Each one kept shroud, nor to his neighbour gave

Or word, or look, or action of despair.   40
Creüs was one; his ponderous iron mace
Lay by him, and a shatter'd rib of rock
Told of his rage, ere he thus sank and pined.
Iapetüs another; in his grasp,
A serpent's plashy neck; its barbed tongue
Squeez'd from the gorge, and all its uncurl'd length
Dead; and because the creature could not spit
Its poison in the eyes of conquering Jove.
Next Cottus: prone he lay, chin uppermost,
As though in pain; for still upon the flint   50
He ground severe his skull, with open mouth
And eyes at horrid working. Nearest him
Asia, born of most enormous Caf,
Who cost her mother Tellus keener pangs
Though feminine, than any of her sons:
More thought than woe was in her dusky face,
For she was prophesying of her glory;
And in her wide imagination stood
Palm-shaded temples, and high rival fanes,
By Oxus or in Ganges' sacred isles.   60
Even as Hope upon her anchor leans,
So leant she, not so fair, upon a tusk
Shed from the broadest of her elephants.
Above her, on a crag's uneasy shelve,
Upon his elbow rais'd, all prostrate else,
Shadow'd Enceladus; once tame and mild
As grazing ox unworried in the meads;
Now tiger-passion'd, lion-thoughted, wroth,
He meditated, plotted, and even now
Was hurling mountains in that second war,   70
Not long delay'd, that scar'd the younger Gods
To hide themselves in forms of beast and bird.
Not far hence Atlas; and beside him prone
Phorcus, the sire of Gorgons. Neighbour'd close

Oceanus, and Tethys, in whose lap
Sobb'd Clymene among her tangled hair.
In midst of all lay Themis, at the feet
Of Ops the queen; all clouded round from sight,
No shape distinguishable, more than when
Thick night confounds the pine-tops with the clouds: 80
And many else whose names may not be told.
For when the Muse's wings are air-ward spread,
Who shall delay her flight? And she must chaunt
Of Saturn, and his guide, who now had climb'd
With damp and slippery footing from a depth
More horrid still. Above a sombre cliff
Their heads appear'd, and up their stature grew
Till on the level height their steps found ease:
Then Thea spread abroad her trembling arms
Upon the precincts of this nest of pain,   90
And sidelong fix'd her eye on Saturn's face:
There saw she direst strife; the supreme God
At war with all the frailty of grief,
Of rage, of fear, anxiety, revenge,
Remorse, spleen, hope, but most of all despair.
Against these plagues he strove in vain; for Fate
Had pour'd a mortal oil upon his head
A disanointing poison: so that Thea,
Affrighted, kept her still, and let him pass
First onwards in, among the fallen tribe.   100

As with us mortal men, the laden heart
Is persecuted more, and fever'd more,
When it is nighing to the mournful house
Where other hearts are sick of the same bruise;
So Saturn, as he walk'd into the midst,
Felt faint, and would have sunk among the rest,
But that he met Enceladus's eye,
Whose mightiness, and awe of him, at once

Came like an inspiration; and he shouted,
'Titans, behold your God!' at which some groan'd;   110
Some started on their feet; some also shouted;
Some wept, some wail'd, all bow'd with reverence;
And Ops, uplifting her black folded veil,
Show'd her pale cheeks, and all her forehead wan,
Her eye-brows thin and jet, and hollow eyes.
There is a roaring in the bleak-grown pines
When Winter lifts his voice; there is a noise
Among immortals when a God gives sign,
With hushing finger, how he means to load
His tongue with the full weight of utterless thought,   120
With thunder, and with music, and with pomp:
Such noise is like the roar of bleak-grown pines;
Which, when it ceases in this mountain'd world,
No other sound succeeds; but ceasing here,
Among these fallen, Saturn's voice therefrom
Grew up like organ, that begins anew
Its strain, when other harmonies, stopt short,
Leave the dinn'd air vibrating silverly.
Thus grew it up—'Not in my own sad breast,
'Which is its own great judge and searcher out,   130
'Can I find reasons why ye should be thus:
'Not in the legend of the first of days,
' Studied from that old spirit-leaved book
'Which starry Uranus with finger bright
'Sav'd from the shores of darkness, when the waves
'Low-ebb'd still hid it up in shallow gloom;—
'And the which book ye know I ever kept
'For my firm-based footstool:—Ah, infirm!
'Not there, nor in sign, symbol, or portent
'Of element, earth, water, air, and fire,—   140
'At war, at peace, or inter-quarrelling
'One against one, or two, or three, or all
'Each several one against the other three,

72

'As fire with air loud warring when rain-floods
'Drown both, and press them both against earth's face.
'Where, finding sulphur, a quadruple wrath
'Unhinges the poor world;—not in that strife,
'Wherefrom I take strange lore, and read it deep,
'Can I find reason why ye should be thus:
'No, no-where can unriddle, though I search,   150
'And pore on Nature's universal scroll
'Even to swooning, why ye, Divinities,
'The first-born of all shap'd and palpable Gods.
'Should cower beneath what, in comparison,
'Is untremendous might. Yet ye are here,
'O'erwhelmed, and spurn'd, and batter'd, ye are here!
'O Titans, shall I say "Arise!"—ye groan:
'Shall I say "Crouch!"—Ye groan. What can I then?
'O Heaven wide! O unseen parent dear!
'What can I? Tell me, all ye brethren Gods,   160
'How we can war, how engine our great wrath!
'O speak your counsel now, for Saturn's ear
'Is all a-hunger'd. Thou, Oceanus,
'Ponderest high and deep; and in thy face
'I see, astonied, that severe content
'Which comes of thought and musing: give us help!'

    So ended Saturn; and the God of the Sea,
Sophist and sage, from no Athenian grove,
But cogitation in his watery shades,
Arose, with locks not oozy, and began,   170
In murmurs, which his first-endeavouring tongue
Caught infant-like from the far-foamed sands.
'O ye, whom wrath consumes! who, passion-stung,
'Writhe at defeat, and nurse your agonies!
'Shut up your senses, stifle up your ears,
'My voice is not a bellows unto ire.
'Yet listen, ye who will, whilst I bring proof

73

'How ye, perforce, must be content to stoop:
'And in the proof much comfort will I give,
'If ye will take that comfort in its truth.   180
'We fall of course of Nature's law, not force
'Of thunder, or of Jove. Great Saturn, thou
'Hast sifted well the atom-universe;
'But for this reason, that thou art the King,
'And only blind from sheer supremacy,
'One avenue was shaded from thine eyes,
'Through which I wandered to eternal truth.
'And first, as thou wast not the first of powers,
'So art thou not the last; it cannot be:
'Thou art not the beginning nor the end.   190
'From Chaos and parental Darkness came
'Light, the first fruits of that intestine broil,
'That sullen ferment, which for wondrous ends
'Was ripening in itself. The ripe hour came,
'And with it Light, and Light, engendering
'Upon its own producer, forthwith touch'd
'The whole enormous matter into Life.
'Upon that very hour, our parentage,
'The Heavens and the Earth, were manifest:
'Then thou first born, and we the giant race,   200
'Found ourselves ruling new and beauteous realms.
'Now comes the pain of truth, to whom 'tis pain;
'O folly! for to bear all naked truths,
'And to envisage circumstance, all calm,
'That is the top of sovereignty. Mark well!
'As Heaven and Earth are fairer, fairer far
'Than Chaos and blank Darkness, though once chiefs;
'And as we show beyond that Heaven and Earth
'In form and shape compact and beautiful,
'In will, in action free, companionship,   210
'And thousand other signs of purer life;
'Soon on our heels a fresh perfection treads,

'A power more strong in beauty, born of us
'And fated to excel us, as we pass
'In glory that old Darkness: nor are we
'Thereby more conquer'd, than by us the rule
'Of shapeless Chaos. Say, doth the dull soil
'Quarrel with the proud forests it hath fed,
'And feedeth still, more comely than itself?
'Can it deny the chiefdom of green groves?   220
'Or shall the tree be envious of the dove
'Because it cooeth, and hath snowy wings
'To wander wherewithal, and find its joys?
'We are such forest-trees, and our fair boughs
'Have bred forth, not pale solitary doves,
'But eagles golden-feather'd, who do tower
'Above us in their beauty, and must reign
'In right thereof; for 'tis the eternal law
'That first in beauty should be first in might:
'Yea, by that law, another race may drive   230
'Our conquerors to mourn as we do now.
'Have ye beheld the young God of the Seas,
'My dispossessor? Have ye seen his face?
'Have ye beheld his chariot, foam'd along
'By noble winged creatures he hath made?
'I saw him on the calmed waters scud,
'With such a glow of beauty in his eyes.
'That it enforced me to bid sad farewell
'To all my empire: farewell sad I took,
'And hither came, to see how dolorous fate   240
'Had wrought upon ye; and how I might best
'Give consolation in this woe extreme.
'Receive the truth, and let it be your balm.'

    Whether through poz'd conviction, or disdain,
They guarded silence, when Oceanus
Left murmuring, what deepest thought can tell?

But so it was, none answer'd for a space,
Save one whom none regarded, Clymene;
And yet she answer'd not, only complain'd,
With hectic lips, and eyes up-looking mild, 250
Thus wording timidly among the fierce:
'O Father, I am here the simplest voice,
'And all my knowledge is that joy is gone,
'And this thing woe crept in among our hearts,
'There to remain for ever, as I fear:
'I would not bode of evil, if I thought
'So weak a creature could turn off the help
'Which by just right should come of mighty Gods;
'Yet let me tell my sorrow, let me tell
'Of what I heard, and how it made me weep, 260
'And know that we had parted from all hope.
'I stood upon a shore, a pleasant shore,
'Where a sweet clime was breathed from a land
'Of fragrance, quietness, and trees, and flowers.
'Full of calm joy it was, as I of grief;
'Too full of joy and soft delicious warmth;
'So that I felt a movement in my heart
'To chide, and to reproach that solitude
'With songs of misery, music of our woes;
'And sat me down, and took a mouthed shell 270
'And murmur'd into it, and made melody—
'O melody no more! for while I sang,
'And with poor skill let pass into the breeze
'The dull shell's echo, from a bowery strand
'Just opposite, an island of the sea,
'There came enchantment with the shifting wind,
'That did both drown and keep alive my ears.
'I threw my shell away upon the sand,
'And a wave filled it, as my sense was fill'd
'With that new blissful golden melody. 280
'A living death was in each gush of sounds,

76

'Each family of rapturous hurried notes,
'That fell, one after one, yet all at once,
'Like pearl beads dropping sudden from their string:
'And then another, then another strain,
'Each like a dove leaving its olive perch,
'With music wing'd instead of silent plumes,
'To hover round my head, and make me sick
'Of joy and grief at once. Grief overcame,
'And I was stopping up my frantic ears,   290
'When, past all hindrance of my trembling hands,
'A voice came sweeter, sweeter than all tune,
'And still it cried, "Apollo! young Apollo!
'"The morning-bright Apollo! Young Apollo!"
'I fled, it follow'd me, and cried "Apollo!"
'O Father, and O Brethren, had ye felt
'Those pains of mine; O Saturn, hadst thou felt,
'Ye would not call this too indulged tongue
'Presumptuous, in thus venturing to be heard.'

    So far her voice flow'd on, like timorous brook   300
That, lingering along a pebbled coast,
Doth fear to meet the sea: but sea it met,
And shudder'd; for the overwhelming voice
Of huge Encaladus swallow'd it in wrath:
The ponderous syllables, like sullen waves
In the half-glutted hollows of reef-rocks,
Came booming thus, while still upon his arm
He lean'd; not rising, from supreme contempt.
'Or shall we listen to the over-wise,
'Or to the over-foolish, Giant-Gods?   310
'Not thunderbolt on thunderbolt, till all
'That rebel Jove's whole armoury were spent,
'Not world on world upon these shoulders piled,
'Could agonize me more than baby-words
'In midst of this dethronement horrible.

'Speak! roar! shout! yell! ye sleepy Titans all.
'Do ye forget the blows, the buffets vile?
'Are ye not smitten by a youngling arm?
'Dost thou forget, sham Monarch of the Waves,
'Thy scalding in the seas? What, have I rous'd   320
'Your spleens with so few simple words as these?
'O joy! for now I see a thousand eyes
'Wide-glaring for revenge!'—As this he said,
He lifted up his stature vast and stood,
Still without intermission speaking thus:
'Now ye are flames, I'll tell you how to burn,
'And purge the ether of our enemies;
'How to feed fierce the crooked stings of fire,
'And singe away the swollen clouds of Jove,   330
'Stifling that puny essence in its tent.
'O let him feel the evil he hath done;
'For though I scorn Oceanus's lore,
'Much pain have I for more than loss of realms:
'The days of peace and slumberous calm are fled;
'Those days all innocent of scathing war,
'When all the fair Existences of heaven
'Came open-eyed to guess what we would speak:—
'That was before our brows were taught to frown,
'Before our lips knew else but solemn sounds;   340
'That was before we knew the winged thing,
'Victory might be lost, or might be won.
'And be ye mindful that Hyperion,
'Our brightest brother, still is undisgraced—
'Hyperion, lo! his radiance is here!'

All eyes were on Enceladus's face,
And they beheld, while still Hyperion's name
Flew from his lips up to the vaulted rocks,
A pallid gleam across his features stern:
Not savage, for he saw full many a God   350

78

Wroth as himself. He look'd upon them all,
And in each face he saw a gleam of light,
But splendider in Saturn's, whose hoar locks
Shone like the bubbling foam about a keel
When the prow sweeps into a midnight cove.
In pale and silver silence they remain'd,
Till suddenly a splendour, like the morn,
Pervaded all the beetling gloomy steeps,
All the sad spaces of oblivion,
And every gulf, and every chasm old,   360
And every height, and every sullen depth,
Voiceless, or hoarse with loud tormented streams:
And all the everlasting cataracts,
And all the headlong torrents far and near,
Mantled before in darkness and huge shade,
Now saw the light and made it terrible.
It was Hyperion:—a granite peak
His bright feet touch'd, and there he stay'd to view
The misery his brilliance had betray'd
To the most hateful seeing of itself.   370
Golden his hair of short Numidian curl,
Regal his shape majestic, a vast shade
In midst of his own brightness, like the bulk
Of Memnon's image at the set of sun
To one who travels from the dusking East:
Sighs, too, as mournful as that Memnon's harp
He utter'd, while his hands contemplative
He press'd together, and in silence stood.
Despondence seiz'd again the fallen Gods
At sight of the dejected King of Day,   380
And many hid their faces from the light:
But fierce Enceladus sent forth his eyes
Among the brotherhood; and, at their glare,
Uprose Iäpetus, and Creüs too,
And Phorcus, sea-born, and together strode

To where he towered on his eminence.
There those four shouted forth old Saturn's name;
Hyperion from the peak loud answered, 'Saturn!'
Saturn sat near the Mother of the Gods,
In whose face was no joy, though all the Gods   390
Gave from their hollow throats the name of 'Saturn!'

BOOK III

THUS in alternate uproar and sad peace,
Amazed were those Titans utterly.
O leave them, Muse! O leave them to their woes;
For thou art weak to sing such tumults dire:
A solitary sorrow best befits
Thy lips, and antheming a lonely grief.
Leave them, O Muse! for thou anon wilt find
Many a fallen old Divinity
Wandering in vain about bewildered shores.
Meantime touch piously the Delphic harp,   10
And not a wind of heaven but will breathe
In aid soft warble from the Dorian flute;
For lo! 'tis for the Father of all verse.
Flush every thing that hath a vermeil hue,
Let the rose glow intense and warm the air,
And let the clouds of even and of morn
Float in voluptuous fleeces o'er the hills;
Let the red wine within the goblet boil,
Cold as a bubbling well; let faint-lipp'd shells,
On sands, or in great deeps, vermilion turn   20
Through all their labyrinths; and let the maid
Blush keenly, as with some warm kiss surpris'd.
Chief isle of the embowered Cyclades,
Rejoice, O Delos, with thine olives green,
And poplars, and lawn-shading palms, and beech,

In which the Zephyr breathes the loudest song,
And hazels thick, dark-stemm'd beneath the shade:
Apollo is once more the golden theme!
Where was he, when the Giant of the Sun
Stood bright, amid the sorrow of his peers? 30
Together had he left his mother fair
And his twin-sister sleeping in their bower,
And in the morning twilight wandered forth
Beside the osiers of a rivulet,
Full ankle-deep in lilies of the vale.
The nightingale had ceas'd, and a few stars
Were lingering in the heavens, while the thrush
Began calm-throated. Throughout all the isle
There was no covert, no retired cave
Unhaunted by the murmurous noise of waves, 40
Though scarcely heard in many a green recess.
He listen'd, and he wept, and his bright tears
Went trickling down the golden bow he held.
Thus with half-shut suffused eyes he stood,
While from beneath some cumbrous boughs hard by
With solemn step an awful Goddess came,
And there was purport in her looks for him,
Which he with eager guess began to read
Perplex'd, the while melodiously he said:
'How cam'st thou over the unfooted sea? 50
'Or hath that antique mien and robed form
'Mov'd in these vales invisible till now?
'Sure I have heard those vestments sweeping o'er
'The fallen leaves, when I have sat alone
'In cool mid-forest. Surely I have traced
'The rustle of those ample skirts about
'These grassy solitudes, and seen the flowers
'Lift up their heads, as still the whisper pass'd.
'Goddess! I have beheld those eyes before,
'And their eternal calm, and all that face, 60

'Or I have dream'd.'—'Yes,' said the supreme shape,
'Thou hast dream'd of me; and awaking up
'Didst find a lyre all golden by thy side,
'Whose strings touch'd by thy fingers, all the vast
'Unwearied ear of the whole universe
'Listen'd in pain and pleasure at the birth
'Of such new tuneful wonder. Is't not strange
'That thou shouldst weep, so gifted? Tell me, youth,
'What sorrow thou canst feel; for I am sad
'When thou dost shed a tear: explain thy griefs   70
'To one who in this lonely isle hath been
'The watcher of thy sleep and hours of life,
'From the young day when first thy infant hand
'Pluck'd witless the weak flowers, till thine arm
'Could bend that bow heroic to all times.
'Show thy heart's secret to an ancient Power
'Who hath forsaken old and sacred thrones
'For prophecies of thee, and for the sake
'Of loveliness new born.'—Apollo then,
With sudden scrutiny and gloomless eyes,   80
Thus answer'd, while his white melodious throat
Throbb'd with the syllables.—'Mnemosyne!
'Thy name is on my tongue, I know not how;
'Why should I tell thee what thou so well seest?
'Why should I strive to show what from thy lips
'Would come to no mystery? For me, dark, dark,
'And painful vile oblivion seals my eyes:
'I strive to search wherefore I am so sad,
'Until a melancholy numbs my limbs:
'And then upon the grass I sit, and moan,   90
'Like one who once had wings.—O why should I
'Feel curs'd and thwarted, when the liegeless air
'Yields to my step aspirant? why should I
'Spurn the green turf as hateful to my feet?
'Goddess benign, point forth some unknown thing:

'Are there not other regions than this isle?
'What are the stars? There is the sun, the sun!
'And the most patient brilliance of the moon!
'And stars by thousands! Point me out the way
'To any one particular beauteous star,   100
'And I will flit into it with my lyre,
'And make its silvery splendour pant with bliss.
'I have heard the cloudy thunder: Where is power?
'Whose hand, whose essence, what divinity
'Makes this alarum in the elements,
'While I here idle listen on the shores
'In fearless yet in aching ignorance?
'O tell me, lonely Goddess, by thy harp
'That waileth every morn and eventide,
'Tell me why thus I rave, about these groves!   110
'Mute thou remainest—Mute! yet I can read
'A wondrous lesson in thy silent face:
'Knowledge enormous makes a God of me.
'Names, deeds, gray legends, dire events, rebellions,
'Majesties, sovran voices, agonies,
'Creations and destroyings, all at once
'Pour into the wide hollows of my brain,
'And deify me, as if some blithe wine
'Or bright elixir peerless I had drunk,
'And so become immortal.'—Thus the God,   120
While his enkindled eyes, with level glance
Beneath his white soft temples, stedfast kept
Trembling with light upon Mnemosyne.
Soon wild commotions shook him, and made flush
All the immortal fairness of his limbs;
Most like the struggle at the gate of death;
Or liker still to one who should take leave
Of pale immortal death, and with a pang
As hot as death's is chill, with fierce convulse
Die into life: so young Apollo anguish'd: 130

83

His very hair, his golden tresses famed
Kept undulation round his eager neck.
During the pain Mnemosyne upheld
Her arms as one who prophesied.—At length
Apollo shriek'd;—and lo! from all his limbs
Celestial . . .

To JAMES AUGUSTUS HESSEY
[*Thursday 8 Oct. 1818*]
My dear Hessey,

   You are very good in sending me the letter from the Chronicle—
and I am very bad in not acknowledging such a kindness sooner.—
pray forgive me.—It has so chanced that I have had that paper
every day—I have seen today's. I cannot but feel indebted to those
Gentlemen who have taken my part—As for the rest, I begin to
get a little acquainted with my own strength and weakness.—Praise
or blame has but a momentary effect on the man whose love of
beauty in the abstract makes him a severe critic on his own Works.
My own domestic criticism has given me pain without comparison
beyond what Blackwood or the Quarterly could possibly inflict.
And also when I feel I am right no external praise can give me such
a glow as my own solitary reperception & ratification of what is
fine. J. S. is perfectly right in regard to the slip-shod Endymion.
That it is so is no fault of mine.—No!—though it may sound a little
paradoxical. It is as good as I had power to make it—by myself—
Had I been nervous about its being a perfect piece, & with that view
asked advice, & trembled over every page, it would not have been
written; for it is not in my nature to fumble—I will write in-
dependantly.—I have written independently *without Judgment.*—I
may write independently, & *with judgment* hereafter.—The Genius
of Poetry must work out its own salvation in a man: It cannot be
matured by law & precept, but by sensation & watchfulness in
itself. That which is creative must create itself—In Endymion, I

leaped headlong into the Sea, and thereby have become better acquainted with the Soundings, the quicksands, & the rocks, than if I had stayed upon the green shore, and piped a silly pipe, and took tea & comfortable advice.—I was never afraid of failure; for I would sooner fail than not be among the greatest—But I am nigh getting into a rant. So, with remembrances to Taylor and Woodhouse &c I am

Yrs very sincerely
John Keats.

To GEORGE AND GEORGIANA KEATS
[*Wednesday 14*] *Oct. 1818*

. . . She is not a Cleopatra; but she is at least a Charmian. She has a rich eastern look; she has fine eyes and fine manners. When she comes into a room she makes an impression the same as the Beauty of a Leopardess. She is too fine and too con[s]cious of her Self to repulse any Man who may address her—from habit she thinks that nothing *particular*. I always find myself more at ease with such a woman; the picture before me always gives me a life and animation which I cannot possibly feel with anything inferiour—I am at such times too much occupied in admiring to be awkward or on a tremble. I forget myself entirely because I live in her. You will by this time think I am in love with her; so before I go any further I will tell you I am not—she kept me awake one Night as a tune of Mozart's might do—I speak of the thing as a passtime and an amuzement than which I can feel none deeper than a conversation with an imperial woman the very 'yes' and 'no' of whose Lips is to me a Banquet. I dont cry to take the moon home with me in my Pocket not [*for* nor] do I fret to leave her behind me. I like her and her like because one has no *sensations*—what we both are is taken for granted—

To GEORGE AND GEORGIANA KEATS
[*Monday 26*] *Oct. 1818*

. . . . Since I wrote thus far I have met with that same Lady again, whom I saw at Hastings and whom I met when we were going to the English Opera. It was in a street which goes from Bedford Row to Lamb's Conduit Street—I passed her and turned back—she seemed glad of it; glad to see me and not offended at my passing her before. We walked on towards Islington where we called on a friend of her's who keeps a Boarding School. She has always been an enigma to me—she has been in a Room with you and with Reynolds and wishes we should be acquainted without any of our common acquaintance knowing it. As we went along, some times through shabby, sometimes through decent Street[s] I had my guessing at work, not knowing what it would be and prepared to meet any surprise—First it ended at this House at Islington: on parting from which I pressed to attend her home. She consented, and then again my thoughts were at work what it might lead to, tho' now they had received a sort of genteel hint from the Boarding School. Our Walk ended in 34 Gloucester Street, Queen Square— not exactly so for we went up stairs into her sitting room—a very tasty sort of place with Books, Pictures a bronze statue of Buona- parte, Music, æolian Harp; a Parrot, a Linnet—a Case of choice Lique[u]rs &c. &c. & she behaved in the kindest manner—made me take home a Grouse for Tom's dinner—Asked for my address for the purpose of sending more game—As I had warmed with her before and kissed her—I though[t] it would be living backwards not to do so again—she had a better taste: she perceived how much a thing of course it was and shrunk from it—not in a prudish way but in as I say a good taste—She cont[r]ived to disappoint me in a way which made me feel more pleasure than a simple kiss could do —she said I should please her much more if I would only press her hand and go away. Whether she was in a different disposition when I saw her before—or whether I have in fancy wrong'd her I cannot

86

tell—I expect to pass some pleasant hours with her now and then: in which I feel I shall be of service to her in matters of knowledge and taste: if I can I will—I have no libidinous thought about her—she and your George are the only women à peu près de mon age whom I would be content to know for their mind and friendship alone. . . .

To RICHARD WOODHOUSE
[*Tuesday 27 Oct. 1818*]
My dear Woodhouse,

Your Letter gave me a great satisfaction; more on account of its friendliness, than any relish of that matter in it which is accounted so acceptable in the 'genus irritabile'. The best answer I can give you is in a clerklike manner to make some observations on two principle points, which seem to point like indices into the midst of the whole pro and con, about genius, and views and atchievements and ambition and cœtera. 1st. As to the poetical Character itself (I mean that sort of which, if I am any thing, I am a Member; that sort distinguished from the wordsworthian or egotistical sublime; which is a thing per se and stands alone) it is not itself—it has no self—it is every thing and nothing—It has no character—it enjoys light and shade; it lives in gusto, be it foul or fair, high or low, rich or poor, mean or elevated—It has as much delight in conceiving an Iago as an Imogen. What shocks the virtuous philosop[h]er, delights the camelion Poet. It does no harm from its relish of the dark side of things any more than from its taste for the bright one; because they both end in speculation. A Poet is the most unpoetical of any thing in existence; because he has no Identity—he is continually in for—and filling some other Body—The Sun, the Moon, the Sea and Men and Women who are creatures of impulse are poetical and have about them an unchangeable attribute—the poet has none; no identity—he is certainly the most unpoetical of all God's Creatures. If then he has no self, and if I am a Poet, where is the Wonder that I should say I would ~~right~~ write no more? Might I

87

not at that very instant have been cogitating on the Characters of saturn and Ops? It is a wretched thing to confess; but is a very fact that not one word I ever utter can be taken for granted as an opinion growing out of my identical nature—how can it, when I have no nature? When I am in a room with People if I ever am free from speculating on creations of my own brain, then not myself goes home to myself: but the identity of every one in the room begins to [*for* so] to press upon me that I am in a very little time an[ni]hilated —not only among Men; it would be the same in a Nursery of children: I know not whether I make myself wholly understood: I hope enough so to let you see that no dependence is to be placed on what I said that day.

In the second place I will speak of my views, and of the life I purpose to myself—I am ambitious of doing the world some good: if I should be spared that may be the work of maturer years—in the interval I will assay to reach to as high a summit in Poetry as the nerve bestowed upon me will suffer. The faint conceptions I have of Poems to come brings the blood frequently into my forehead— All I hope is that I may not lose all interest in human affairs—that the solitary indifference I feel for applause even from the finest Spirits, will not blunt any acuteness of vision I may have. I do not think it will—I feel assured I should write from the mere yearning and fondness I have for the Beautiful even if my night's labours should be burnt every morning, and no eye ever shine upon them. But even now I am perhaps not speaking from myself: but from some character in whose soul I now live. I am sure however that this next sentence is from myself. I feel your anxiety, good opinion and friendliness in the highest degree, and am

Your's most sincerely

John Keats

To GEORGE AND GEORGIANA KEATS
Friday [*18 Dec.*] *1818*

. . . . Shall I give you Miss Brawn[e]? She is about my height—
with a fine style of countenance of the lengthen'd sort—she wants
sentiment in every feature—she manages to make her hair look well
—her nostrills are fine—though a little painful—he[r] mouth is bad
and good—he[r] Profil is better than her full-face which indeed is
not full put [*for* but] pale and thin without showing any bone—
Her shape is very graceful and so are her movements—her Arms
are good her hands badish—her feet tolerable—she is not seventeen
—but she is ignorant—monstrous in her behaviour flying out in all
directions, calling people such names—that I was forced lately to
make use of the term *Minx*—this is I think no[t] from any innate
vice but from a penchant she has for acting stylishly. I am however
tired of such style and shall decline any more of it. . . .

Ode

Bards of Passion and of Mirth

BARDS of Passion and of Mirth,
Ye have left your souls on earth!
Have ye souls in heaven too,
Double-lived in regions new?
Yes, and those of heaven commune
With the spheres of sun and moon;
With the noise of fountains wond'rous,
And the parle of voices thund'rous;
With the whisper of heaven's trees
And one another, in soft ease   10

Seated on Elysian lawns
Brows'd by none but Dian's fawns
Underneath large blue-bells tented,
Where the daisies are rose-scented,
And the rose herself has got
Perfume which on earth is not;
Where the nightingale doth sing
Not a senseless, tranced thing,
But divine melodious truth;
Philosophic numbers smooth;   20
Tales and golden histories
Of heaven and its mysteries.

Thus ye live on high, and then
On the earth ye live again;
And the souls ye left behind you
Teach us, here, the way to find you,
Where your other souls are joying,
Never slumber'd, never cloying.
Here, your earth-born souls still speak
To mortals, of their little week;   30
Of their sorrows and delights;
Of their passions and their spites;
Of their glory and their shame;
What does strengthen and what maim.
Thus ye teach us, every day,
Wisdom, though fled far away.

Bards of Passion and of Mirth,
Ye have left your souls on earth!
Ye have souls in heaven too,
Double-lived in regions new!   40

Fancy

EVER let the Fancy roam,
Pleasure never is at home:
At a touch sweet Pleasure melteth,
Like to bubbles when rain pelteth;
Then let winged Fancy wander
Through the thought still spread beyond her:
Open wide the mind's cage-door,
She'll dart forth, and cloudward soar.
O sweet Fancy! let her loose;
Summer's joys are spoilt by use,   10
And the enjoying of the Spring
Fades as does its blossoming;
Autumn's red-lipp'd fruitage too,
Blushing through the mist and dew,
Cloys with tasting: What do then?
Sit thee by the ingle, when
The sear faggot blazes bright,
Spirit of a winter's night;
When the soundless earth is muffled,
And the caked snow is shuffled   20
From the ploughboy's heavy shoon;
When the Night doth meet the Noon
In a dark conspiracy
To banish Even from her sky.
Sit thee there, and send abroad,
With a mind self-overaw'd,
Fancy, high-commission'd:—send her!
She has vassals to attend her:
She will bring, in spite of frost,

Beauties that the earth hath lost   30
She will bring thee, all together,
All delights of summer weather;
All the buds and bells of May,
From dewy sward or thorny spray
All the heaped Autumn's wealth,
With a still, mysterious stealth:
She will mix these pleasures up
Like three fit wines in a cup,
And thou shalt quaff it:—thou shalt hear
Distant harvest-carols clear;   40
Rustle of the reaped corn;
Sweet birds antheming the morn:
And, in the same moment—hark!
'Tis the early April lark,
Or the rooks, with busy caw,
Foraging for sticks and straw.
Thou shalt, at one glance, behold
The daisy and the marigold;
White-plum'd lilies, and the first
Hedge-grown primrose that hath burst;   50
Shaded hyacinth, alway
Sapphire queen of the mid-May;
And every leaf, and every flower
Pearled with the self-same shower.
Thou shalt see the field-mouse peep
Meagre from its celled sleep;
And the snake all winter-thin
Cast on sunny bank its skin;
Freckled nest-eggs thou shalt see
Hatching in the hawthorn-tree,   60
When the hen-bird's wing doth rest
Quiet on her mossy nest;
Then the hurry and alarm
When the bee-hive casts its swarm;

Acorns ripe down-pattering,
While the autumn breezes sing.

Oh, sweet Fancy! let her loose;
Every thing is spoilt by use:
Where's the cheek that doth not fade,
Too much gaz'd at? Where's the maid   70
Whose lip mature is ever new?
Where's the eye, however blue,
Doth not weary? Where's the face
One would meet in every place?
Where's the voice, however soft,
One would hear so very oft?
At a touch sweet Pleasure melteth
Like to bubbles when rain pelteth.
Let, then, winged Fancy find
Thee a mistress to thy mind: 80
Dulcet-eyed as Ceres' daughter,
Ere the God of Torment taught her
How to frown and how to chide;
With a waist and with a side
White as Hebe's, when her zone
Slipt its golden clasp, and down
Fell her kirtle to her feet,
While she held the goblet sweet,
And Jove grew languid.—Break the mesh
Of the Fancy's silken leash;   90
Quickly break her prison-string
And such joys as these she'll bring.—
Let the winged Fancy roam
Pleasure never is at home.

The Eve of St. Agnes

I

ST. AGNES' EVE—Ah, bitter chill it was!
The owl, for all his feathers, was a-cold;
The hare limp'd trembling through the frozen grass,
And silent was the flock in woolly fold:
Numb were the Beadsman's fingers, while he told
His rosary, and while his frosted breath,
Like pious incense from a censer old,
Seem'd taking flight for heaven, without a death,
Past the sweet Virgin's picture, while his prayer he saith.

II

His prayer he saith, this patient, holy man;   10
Then takes his lamp, and riseth from his knees,
And back returneth, meagre, barefoot, wan,
Along the chapel aisle by slow degrees:
The sculptur'd dead, on each side, seem to freeze,
Emprison'd in black, purgatorial rails:
Knights, ladies, praying in dumb orat'ries,
He passeth by; and his weak spirit fails
To think how they may ache in icy hoods and mails.

III

Northward he turneth through a little door,
And scarce three steps, ere Music's golden tongue   20
Flatter'd to tears this aged man and poor;
But no—already had his deathbell rung;
The joys of all his life were said and sung:
His was harsh penance on St. Agnes' Eve:
Another way he went, and soon among

Rough ashes sat he for his soul's reprieve,
And all night kept awake, for sinners' sake to grieve.

IV

That ancient Beadsman heard the prelude soft;
And so it chanc'd, for many a door was wide,
From hurry to and fro. Soon, up aloft,   30
The silver, snarling trumpets 'gan to chide:
The level chambers, ready with their pride,
Were glowing to receive a thousand guests:
The carved angels, ever eager-eyed,
Star'd, where upon their heads the cornice rests,
With hair blown back, and wings put cross-wise on their breasts.

V

At length burst in the argent revelry,
With plume, tiara, and all rich array,
Numerous as shadows haunting fairily
The brain, new stuff'd, in youth, with triumphs gay   40
Of old romance. These let us wish away,
And turn, sole-thoughted, to one Lady there,
Whose heart had brooded, all that wintry day,
On love, and wing'd St. Agnes' saintly care,
As she had heard old dames full many times declare.

VI

They told her how, upon St. Agnes' Eve,
Young virgins might have visions of delight,
And soft adorings from their loves receive
Upon the honey'd middle of the night,
If ceremonies due they did aright;   50
As, supperless to bed they must retire,
And couch supine their beauties, lily white;
Nor look behind, nor sideways, but require
Of Heaven with upward eyes for all that they desire.

VII

Full of this whim was thoughtful Madeline:
The music, yearning like a God in pain,
She scarcely heard: her maiden eyes divine,
Fix'd on the floor, saw many a sweeping train
Pass by—she heeded not at all: in vain
Came many a tiptoe, amorous cavalier,   60
And back retir'd; not cool'd by high disdain,
But she saw not: her heart was otherwhere:
She sigh'd for Agnes' dreams, the sweetest of the year.

VIII

She danc'd along with vague, regardless eyes,
Anxious her lips, her breathing quick and short:
The hallow'd hour was near at hand: she sighs
Amid the timbrels, and the throng'd resort
Of whisperers in anger, or in sport;
'Mid looks of love, defiance, hate, and scorn,
Hoodwink'd with faery fancy; all amort,   70
Save to St. Agnes and her lambs unshorn,
And all the bliss to be before to-morrow morn.

IX

So, purposing each moment to retire,
She linger'd still. Meantime, across the moors,
Had come young Porphyro, with heart on fire
For Madeline. Beside the portal doors,
Buttress'd from moonlight, stands he, and implores
All saints to give him sight of Madeline,
But for one moment in the tedious hours,
That he might gaze and worship all unseen;   80
Perchance speak, kneel, touch, kiss—in sooth such things have been.

X

He ventures in: let not buzz'd whisper tell:
All eyes be muffled, or a hundred swords

Will storm his heart, Love's fev'rous citadel:
For him, those chambers held barbarian hordes,
Hyena foemen, and hot-blooded lords,
Whose very dogs would execrations howl
Against his lineage: not one breast affords
Him any mercy, in that mansion foul,
Save one old beldame, weak in body and in soul.   90

XI

Ah, happy chance! the aged creature came,
Shuffling along with ivory-headed wand,
To where he stood, hid from the torch's flame,
Behind a broad hall-pillar, far beyond
The sound of merriment and chorus bland:
He startled her; but soon she knew his face
And grasp'd his fingers in her palsied hand,
Saying, 'Mercy, Porphyro! hie thee from this place;
'They are all here to-night, the whole blood-thirsty race!

XII

'Get hence! get hence! there's dwarfish Hildebrand;   100
'He had a fever late, and in the fit
'He cursed thee and thine, both house and land:
'Then there's that old Lord Maurice, not a whit
'More tame for his gray hairs—Alas me! flit!
'Flit like a ghost away.'—'Ah, Gossip dear,
'We're safe enough; here in this arm-chair sit,
'And tell me how'—'Good Saints! not here, not here;
'Follow me, child, or else these stones will be thy bier.'

XIII

He followed through a lowly arched way,
Brushing the cobwebs with his lofty plume,   110
And as she mutter'd 'Well-a—well-a-day!'
He found him in a little moonlight room,

Pale, lattic'd, chill, and silent as a tomb.
'Now tell me where is Madeline,' said he,
'O tell me, Angela, by the holy loom
'Which none but secret sisterhood may see,
'When they St. Agnes' wool are weaving piously.'

XIV

'St. Agnes! Ah! it is St. Agnes' Eve—
'Yet men will murder upon holy days:
'Thou must hold water in a witch's sieve,   120
'And be liege-lord of all the Elves and Fays,
'To venture so: it fills me with amaze
'To see thee, Porphyro!—St. Agnes' Eve!
'God's help! my lady fair the conjuror plays
'This very night: good angels her deceive!
'But let me laugh awhile, I've mickle time to grieve.'

XV

Feebly she laugheth in the languid moon,
While Porphyro upon her face doth look,
Like puzzled urchin on an aged crone
Who keepeth clos'd a wond'rous riddle-book,   130
As spectacled she sits in chimney nook.
But soon his eyes grew brilliant, when she told
His lady's purpose; and he scarce could brook
Tears, at the thought of those enchantments cold
And Madeline asleep in lap of legends old.

XVI

Sudden a thought came like a full-blown rose,
Flushing his brow, and in his pained heart
Made purple riot: then doth he propose
A stratagem, that makes the beldame start:
'A cruel man and impious thou art: 140
'Sweet lady, let her pray, and sleep, and dream
'Alone with her good angels, far apart

'From wicked men like thee. Go, go!—I deem
'Thou canst not surely be the same that thou didst seem.'

XVII

'I will not harm her, by all saints I swear,'
Quoth Porphyro: 'O may I ne'er find grace
'When my weak voice shall whisper its last prayer,
'If one of her soft ringlets I displace,
'Or look with ruffian passion in her face:
'Good Angela, believe me by these tears;   150
'Or I will, even in a moment's space,
'Awake, with horrid shout, my foemen's ears,
'And beard them, though they be more fang'd than wolves and
    bears.'

XVIII

'Ah, why wilt thou affright a feeble soul?
'A poor, weak, palsy-stricken, churchyard thing,
'Whose passing-bell may ere the midnight toll;
'Whose prayers for thee, each morn and evening,
'Were never miss'd.'—Thus plaining, doth she bring
A gentler speech from burning Porphyro;
So woful, and of such deep sorrowing,   160
    That Angela gives promise she will do
Whatever he shall wish, betide her weal or woe.

XIX

Which was, to lead him, in close secrecy,
Even to Madeline's chamber, and there hide
Him in a closet, of such privacy
That he might see her beauty unespied,
And win perhaps that night a peerless bride,
While legion'd fairies pac'd the coverlet
And pale enchantment held her sleepy-eyed.
Never on such a night have lovers met,   170
Since Merlin paid his Demon all the monstrous debt.

XX

'It shall be as thou wishest,' said the Dame:
'All cates and dainties shall be stored there
'Quickly on this feast-night: by the tambour frame
'Her own lute thou wilt see: no time to spare,
'For I am slow and feeble, and scarce dare
'On such a catering trust my dizzy head.
'Wait here, my child, with patience; kneel in prayer
'The while: Ah! thou must needs the lady wed,
'Or may I never leave my grave among the dead.'   180

XXI

So saying, she hobbled off with busy fear.
The lover's endless minutes slowly pass'd;
The dame return'd, and whisper'd in his ear
To follow her; with aged eyes aghast,
From fright of dim espial. Safe at last,
Through many a dusky gallery, they gain
The maiden's chamber, silken, hush'd, and chaste;
Where Porphyro took covert, pleas'd amain.
His poor guide hurried back with agues in her brain.

XXII

Her falt'ring hand upon the balustrade,   190
Old Angela was feeling for the stair,
When Madeline, St. Agnes' charmed maid,
Rose, like a mission'd spirit, unaware:
With silver taper's light, and pious care,
She turn'd, and down the aged gossip led
To a safe level matting. Now prepare,
Young Porphyro, for gazing on that bed;
She comes, she comes again, like ring-dove fray'd and fled.

XXIII

Out went the taper as she hurried in;
Its little smoke, in pallid moonshine, died: 200

She clos'd the door, she panted, all akin
To spirits of the air, and visions wide:
No uttered syllable, or, woe betide!
But to her heart, her heart was voluble,
Paining with eloquence her balmy side;
As though a tongueless nightingale should swell
Her throat in vain, and die, heart-stifled, in her dell.

XXIV

A casement high and triple-arch'd there was,
All garlanded with carven imag'ries
Of fruits, and flowers, and bunches of knot-grass,   210
And diamonded with panes of quaint device,
Innumerable of stains and splendid dyes,
As are the tiger-moth's deep-damask'd wings;
And in the midst, 'mong thousand heraldries,
And twilight saints, and dim emblazonings,
A shielded scutcheon blush'd with blood of queens and kings.

XXV

Full on this casement shone the wintry moon,
And threw warm gules on Madeline's fair breast,
As down she knelt for heaven's grace and boon;
Rose-bloom fell on her hands, together prest,   220
And on her silver cross soft amethyst,
And on her hair a glory, like a saint:
She seem'd a splendid angel, newly drest,
Save wings, for heaven:—Porphyro grew faint:
She knelt, so pure a thing, so free from mortal taint.

XXVI

Anon his heart revives: her vespers done,
Of all its wreathed pearls her hair she frees;
Unclasps her warmed jewels one by one;
Loosens her fragrant boddice; by degrees

Her rich attire creeps rustling to her knees: 230
  Half-hidden, like a mermaid in sea-weed,
Pensive awhile she dreams awake, and sees,
  In fancy, fair St. Agnes in her bed,
But dares not look behind, or all the charm is fled.

XXVII

Soon, trembling in her soft and chilly nest,
  In sort of wakeful swoon, perplex'd she lay,
Until the poppied warmth of sleep oppress'd
  Her soothed limbs, and soul fatigued away;
Flown, like a thought, until the morrow-day;
  Blissfully haven'd both from joy and pain;   240
Clasp'd like a missal where swart Paynims pray;
  Blinded alike from sunshine and from rain,
As though a rose should shut, and be a bud again.

XXVIII

Stol'n to this paradise, and so entranced,
  Porphyro gazed upon her empty dress,
And listen'd to her breathing, if it chanced
  To wake into a slumberous tenderness;
Which when he heard, that minute did he bless,
  And breath'd himself: then from the closet crept,
Noiseless as fear in a wide wilderness,   250
  And over the hush'd carpet, silent, stept,
And 'tween the curtains peep'd, where, lo!—how fast she slept.

XXIX

Then by the bed-side, where the faded moon
  Made a dim, silver twilight, soft he set
A table, and, half anguish'd, threw thereon
  A cloth of woven crimson, gold, and jet:—
O for some drowsy Morphean amulet!
  The boisterous, midnight, festive clarion,

The kettle-drum, and far-heard clarionet,
  Affray his ears, though but in dying tone:—   260
The hall door shuts again, and all the noise is gone.

XXX

And still she slept an azure-lidded sleep,
  In blanched linen, smooth, and lavender'd,
While he from forth the closet brought a heap
  Of candied apple, quince, and plum, and gourd
  With jellies soother than the creamy curd,
And lucent syrops, tinct with cinnamon;
  Manna and dates, in argosy transferr'd
From Fez; and spiced dainties, every one,
From silken Samarcand to cedar'd Lebanon.   270

XXXI

These delicates he heap'd with glowing hand
  On golden dishes and in baskets bright
Of wreathed silver: sumptuous they stand
  In the retired quiet of the night,
  Filling the chilly room with perfume light.—
'And now, my love, my seraph fair, awake!
  'Thou art my heaven, and I thine eremite:
'Open thine eyes, for meek St. Agnes' sake,
'Or shall I drowse beside thee, so my soul doth ache.'

XXXII

Thus whispering, his warm, unnerved arm   280
  Sank in her pillow. Shaded was her dream
By the dusk curtains:—'twas a midnight charm
  Impossible to melt as iced stream:
  The lustrous salvers in the moonlight gleam;
Broad golden fringe upon the carpet lies:
  It seem'd he never, never could redeem
From such a stedfast spell his lady's eyes;
So mus'd awhile, entoil'd in woofed phantasies.

XXXIII

Awakening up, he took her hollow lute,—
Tumultuous,—and, in chords that tenderest be,   290
He play'd an ancient ditty, long since mute,
In Provence call'd, 'La belle dame sans mercy':
Close to her ear touching the melody;—
Wherewith disturb'd, she utter'd a soft moan:
He ceased—she panted quick—and suddenly
Her blue affrayed eyes wide open shone:
Upon his knees he sank, pale as smooth-sculptured stone.

XXXIV

Her eyes were open, but she still beheld,
Now wide awake, the vision of her sleep:
There was a painful change, that nigh expell'd   300
The blisses of her dream so pure and deep
At which fair Madeline began to weep,
And moan forth witless words with many a sigh;
While still her gaze on Porphyro would keep;
Who knelt, with joined hands and piteous eye,
Fearing to move or speak, she look'd so dreamingly.

XXXV

'Ah, Porphyro!' said she, 'but even now
'Thy voice was at sweet tremble in mine ear,
'Made tuneable with every sweetest vow;
'And those sad eyes were spiritual and clear: 310
'How chang'd thou art! how pallid, chill, and drear!
'Give me that voice again, my Porphyro,
'Those looks immortal, those complainings dear!
'O leave me not in this eternal woe,
'For if thou diest, my Love, I know not where to go.'

XXXVI

Beyond a mortal man impassion'd far
At these voluptuous accents, he arose,

Ethereal, flush'd, and like a throbbing star
Seen mid the sapphire heaven's deep repose
Into her dream he melted, as the rose   320
Blendeth its odour with the violet,—
Solution sweet: meantime the frost-wind blows
Like Love's alarum pattering the sharp sleet
Against the window-panes; St. Agnes' moon hath set.

XXXVII

'Tis dark: quick pattereth the flaw-blown sleet:
'This is no dream, my bride, my Madeline!'
'Tis dark: the iced gusts still rave and beat:
'No dream, alas! alas! and woe is mine!
'Porphyro will leave me here to fade and pine.—
'Cruel! what traitor could thee hither bring?   330
'I curse not, for my heart is lost in thine
'Though thou forsakest a deceived thing;—
'A dove forlorn and lost with sick unpruned wing.'

XXXVIII

'My Madeline! sweet dreamer! lovely bride!
'Say, may I be for aye thy vassal blest?
'Thy beauty's shield, heart-shap'd and vermeil dyed?
'Ah, silver shrine, here will I take my rest
'After so many hours of toil and quest,
'A famish'd pilgrim,—saved by miracle.
'Though I have found, I will not rob thy nest   340
'Saving of thy sweet self; if thou think'st well
'To trust, fair Madeline, to no rude infidel.'

XXXIX

'Hark! 'tis an elfin-storm from faery land,
'Of haggard seeming, but a boon indeed:
'Arise—arise! the morning is at hand;—
'The bloated wassaillers will never heed:—

'Let us away, my love, with happy speed;
'There are no ears to hear, or eyes to see,—
'Drown'd all in Rhenish and the sleepy mead:
'Awake! arise! my love, and fearless be,   350
'For o'er the southern moors I have a home for thee.'

XL

She hurried at his words, beset with fears,
For there were sleeping dragons all around,
At glaring watch, perhaps, with ready spears—
Down the wide stairs a darkling way they found.—
In all the house was heard no human sound.
A chain-droop'd lamp was flickering by each door;
The arras, rich with horseman, hawk, and hound,
Flutter'd in the besieging wind's uproar;
And the long carpets rose along the gusty floor.   360

XLI

They glide, like phantoms, into the wide hall;
Like phantoms, to the iron porch, they glide;
Where lay the Porter, in uneasy sprawl,
With a huge empty flaggon by his side:
The wakeful bloodhound rose and shook his hide,
But his sagacious eye an inmate owns:
By one, and one, the bolts full easy slide:—
The chains lie silent on the footworn stones;—
The key turns, and the door upon its hinges groans.

XLII

And they are gone: ay, ages long ago   370
These lovers fled away into the storm.
That night the Baron dreamt of many a woe,
And all his warrior-guests, with shade and form
Of witch, and demon, and large coffin-worm,
Were long be-nightmar'd. Angela the old

Died palsy-twitch'd, with meagre face deform;
    The Beadsman, after thousand aves told,
For aye unsought for slept among his ashes cold.

The Eve of St. Mark

UPON a Sabbath-day it fell;
Twice holy was the Sabbath-bell,
That call'd the folk to evening prayer;
The city streets were clean and fair
From wholesome drench of April rains;
And, on the western window panes,
The chilly sunset faintly told
Of unmatured green vallies cold,
Of the green thorny bloomless hedge,
Of rivers new with spring-tide sedge,   10
Of primroses by shelter'd rills,
And daisies on the aguish hills.
Twice holy was the Sabbath-bell;
The silent streets were crowded well
With staid and pious companies,
Warm from their fire-side orat'ries;
And moving, with demurest air,
To even-song and vesper prayer.
Each arched porch, and entry low,
Was fill'd with patient folk and slow,   20
With whispers hush, and shuffling feet,
While play'd the organ loud and sweet.

The bells had ceased, the prayers begun,
And Bertha had not yet half done
A curious volume, patch'd and torn,
That all day long, from earliest morn,

Had taken captive her two eyes,
Among its golden broideries;
Perplex'd her with a thousand things,—
The stars of Heaven, and angels' wings,   30
Martyrs in a fiery blaze,
Azure saints in silver rays,
Aaron's breastplate, and the seven
Candlesticks John saw in Heaven,
The winged Lion of Saint Mark,
And the Covenantal Ark,
With its many mysteries,
Cherubim and golden mice.

Bertha was a maiden fair,
Dwelling in the old Minster-square;   40
From her fire-side she could see,
Sidelong, its rich antiquity,
Far as the Bishop's garden-wall;
Where sycamores and elm-trees tall,
Full-leaved, the forest had outstript,
By no sharp north-wind ever nipt,
So shelter'd by the mighty pile.
Bertha arose, and read awhile,
With forehead 'gainst the window-pane.
Again she tried, and then again,   50
Until the dusk eve left her dark
Upon the legend of St. Mark.
From plaited lawn-frill, fine and thin,
She lifted up her soft warm chin,
With aching neck and swimming eyes,
And dazed with saintly imag'ries.

All was gloom, and silent all,
Save now and then the still foot-fall
Of one returning homewards late,
Past the echoing minster-gate.   60

The clamorous daws, that all the day
Above tree-tops and towers play,
Pair by pair had gone to rest,
Each in its ancient belfry-nest,
Where asleep they fall betimes,
To music of the drowsy chimes.

All was silent, all was gloom,
Abroad and in the homely room:
Down she sat, poor cheated soul!
And struck a lamp from the dismal coal;   70
Leaned forward, with bright drooping hair
And slant book, full against the glare.
Her shadow in uneasy guise,
Hover'd about, a giant size,
On ceiling-beam and old oak chair,
The parrot's cage, and panel square;
And the warm angled winter screen,
On which were many monsters seen,
Call'd doves of Siam, Lima mice,
And legless birds of Paradise,   80
Macaw, and tender Av'davat,
And silken-furr'd Angora cat.
Untired she read, her shadow still
Glower'd about, as it would fill
The room with wildest forms and shades,
As though some ghostly queen of spades
Had come to mock behind her back,
And dance, and ruffle her garments black
Untired she read the legend page,
Of holy Mark, from youth to age,   90
On land, on sea, in pagan chains,
Rejoicing for his many pains.
Sometimes the learned eremite,

With golden star, or dagger bright,
Referr'd to pious poesies
Written in smallest crow-quill size
Beneath the text; and thus the rhyme
Was parcell'd out from time to time:
'Gif ye wol stonden hardie wight—
Amiddes of the blacke night—   100
Righte in the churche porch, pardie
Ye wol behold a companie
Appouchen thee full dolourouse
For sooth to sain from everich house
Be it in City or village
Wol come the Phantom and image
Of ilka gent and ilka carle
Whom coldè Deathè hath in parle
And wol some day that very year
Touchen with foulè venime speare   110
And sadly do them all to die—
Hem all shalt thou see verilie—
And everichon shall by the[e] pass
All who must die that year Alas'
—'Als writith he of swevenis,
Men han beforne they wake in bliss,
Whanne that hir friendes thinke hem bound
In crimped shroude farre under grounde;
And how a litling child mote be   120
A saint er its nativitie,
Gif that the modre (God her blesse!)
Kepen in solitarinesse,
And kissen devoute the holy croce.
Of Goddes love, and Sathan's force,—
He writith; and thinges many mo:
Of swiche thinges I may not show.
Bot I must tellen verilie
Somdel of Saintè Cicilie,

And chieflie what he auctorethe
Of Saintè Markis̀ life and dethe:'

At length her constant eyelids come
Upon the fervent martyrdom;
Then lastly to his holy shrine,
Exalt amid the tapers' shine
At Venice,—

To GEORGE AND GEORGIANA KEATS
Friday 19 March 1819

... Neither Poetry, nor Ambition, nor Love have any alertness of countenance as they pass by me: they seem rather like three figures on a greek vase—a Man and two women—whom no one but myself could distinguish in their disguisement. I have this moment received a note from Haslam in which he expects the death of his Father who has been for some time in a state of insensibility—his mother bears up he says very well—I shall go to town tommorrow to see him. This is the world—thus we cannot expect to give way many hours to pleasure—Circumstances are like Clouds continually gathering and bursting—While we are laughing the seed of some trouble is put into the wide arable land of events—while we are laughing it sprouts is [for it] grows and suddenly bears a poison fruit which we must pluck—Even so we have leisure to reason on the misfortunes of our friends; our own touch us too nearly for words. Very few men have ever arrived at a complete disinterestedness of Mind: very few have been influenced by a pure desire of the benefit of others—in the greater part of the Benefactors of & to Humanity some meretricious motive has sullied their greatness—some melodramatic scenery has fa[s]cinated them—From the manner in which I feel Haslam's misfortune I perceive how far I am from any humble standard of disinterestedness—Yet this feeling ought to be carried to its highest pitch as there is no fear of its ever injuring society— which it would do I fear pushed to an extremity—For in wild nature the Hawk would loose his Breakfast of Robins and the Robin his of Worms. The Lion must starve as well as the swallow— The greater part of Men make their way with the same instinctiveness, the same unwandering eye from their purposes, the same animal eagerness as the Hawk—The Hawk wants a Mate, so does the Man—look at them both they set about it and procure on[e] in the same manner—They want both a nest and they both set about one in the same manner—they get their food in the same manner— The noble animal Man for his amusement smokes his pipe—the Hawk balances about the Clouds—that is the only difference of their leisures. This it is that makes the Amusement of Life—to a speculative Mind. I go among the Feilds and catch a glimpse of a stoat or a fieldmouse peeping out of the withered grass—the creature hath a purpose and its eyes are bright with it—I go amongst the buildings of a city and I see a Man hurrying along—to what? the Creature has a purpose and his eyes are bright with it. But then as Wordsworth says, "we have all one human heart"—there is an ellectric fire in human nature tending to purify—so that among these human creature[s] there is continu[a]lly some birth of new heroism—The pity is that we must wonder at it: as we should at finding a pearl in rubbish—I have no doubt that thousands of people never heard of have had hearts comp[l]etely disinterested: I can remember but two—Socrates and Jesus—their Histories evince it— What I heard a little time ago, Taylor observe with respect to Socrates may be said of Jesus—That he was so great a man that though he transmitted no writing of his own to posterity, we have his Mind and his sayings and his greatness handed to us by others. It is to be lamented that the history of the latter was written and revised by Men interested in the pious frauds of Religion. Yet through all this I see his splendour. Even here though I myself am pursueing the same instinctive course as the veriest human animal you can think of—I am however young writing at random—straining at particles of light in the midst of a great darkness—without knowing the bearing of any one assertion of any one opinion. Yet may I not in this be free from sin? May there not be superior beings amused with any graceful, though instinctive attitude my mind m[a]y fall into, as I am entertained with the alertness of a Stoat or the anxiety of a Deer? Though a quarrel in the streets is a thing to be hated, the energies displayed in it are fine; the commonest Man shows a grace in his quarrel—By a superior being our reasoning[s] may take the same tone—though erroneous they may be fine— This is the very thing in which consists poetry; and if so it is not so fine a thing as philosophy—For the same reason that an eagle is not so fine ə thing as a truth— . . .

Bright Star

(Final Version)

BRIGHT star! would I were steadfast as thou art—
  Not in lone splendour hung aloft the night
And watching, with eternal lids apart,
  Like nature's patient, sleepless Eremite,
The moving waters at their priestlike task
  Of pure ablution round earth's human shores,
Or gazing on the new soft fallen mask
  Of snow upon the mountains and the moors—
No—yet still steadfast, still unchangeable,
  Pillow'd upon my fair love's ripening breast,   10
To feel for ever its soft fall and swell,
  Awake for ever in a sweet unrest,
Still, still to hear her tender-taken breath,
And so live ever—or else swoon to death.

To GEORGE AND GEORGIANA KEATS
[*Friday 16 April*] *1819*

. . . The fifth canto of Dante pleases me more and more—it is that one in which he meets with Paulo and Franchesca—I had passed many days in rather a low state of mind, and in the midst of them I dreamt of being in that region of Hell. The dream was one of the most delightful enjoyments I ever had in my life—I floated about the whirling atmosphere as it is described with a beautiful figure to whose lips mine were joined at [*for as*] it seem'd for an age—and in the midst of all this cold and darkness I was warm— even flowery tree tops sprung up and we rested on them sometimes with the lightness of a cloud till the wind blew us away again—I tried a Sonnet upon it—there are fourteen lines but nothing of what I felt in it—o that I could dream it every night— . . .

On a Dream

As Hermes once took to his feathers light,
　　When lulled Argus, baffled, swoon'd and slept,
So on a Delphic reed, my idle spright
　　So play'd, so charm'd, so conquer'd, so bereft
The dragon-world of all its hundred eyes;
　　And, seeing it asleep, so fled away,
Not to pure Ida with its snow-cold skies,
　　Nor unto Tempe, where Jove griev'd that day;
But to that second circle of sad hell,
　　Where in the gust, the whirlwind, and the flaw   10
Of rain and hail-stones, lovers need not tell
Their sorrows—pale were the sweet lips I saw,
Pale were the lips I kiss'd, and fair the form
I floated with, about that melancholy storm.

La Belle Dame sans Merci

I

O WHAT can ail thee, knight-at-arms,
  Alone and palely loitering?
The sedge has wither'd from the lake,
  And no birds sing.

II

O what can ail thee, knight-at-arms,
  So haggard and so woe-begone?
The squirrel's granary is full,
  And the harvest's done.

III

I see a lilly on thy brow,
  With anguish moist and fever dew,   10
And on thy cheeks a fading rose
  Fast withereth too.

IV

I met a lady in the meads,
  Full beautiful—a faery's child,
Her hair was long, her foot was light,
  And her eyes were wild.

V

I made a garland for her head,
  And bracelets too, and fragrant zone;
She look'd at me as she did love,
  And made sweet moan.   20

VI

I set her on my pacing steed,
  And nothing else saw all day long,
For sidelong would she bend, and sing
  A faery's song.

She found me roots of relish sweet,
  And honey wild, and manna dew,
And sure in language strange she said—
  'I love thee true'.

She took me to her elfin grot,
  And there she wept, and sigh'd full sore,   30
And there I shut her wild wild eyes
  With kisses four.

And there she lulled me asleep,
  And there I dream'd—Ah! woe betide!
The latest dream I ever dream'd
  On the cold hill side.

I saw pale kings and princes too,
  Pale warriors, death-pale were they all;
They cried—'La Belle Dame sans Merci
  Hath thee in thrall!'   40

I saw their starved lips in the gloam,
  With horrid warning gaped wide,
And I awoke and found me here,
  On the cold hill's side.

And this is why I sojourn here,
  Alone and palely loitering,
Though the sedge has wither'd from the lake,
  And no birds sing.

To GEORGE AND GEORGIANA KEATS
Wednesday [*21 April 1819*]

... The common cognomen of this world among the misguided
and superstitious is 'a vale of tears' from which we are to be
redeemed by a certain arbitrary interposition of God and taken to
Heaven—What a little circumscribe[d] straightened notion! Call
the world if you Please "The vale of Soul-making". Then you will
find out the use of the world (I am speaking now in the highest
terms for human nature admitting it to be immortal which I will
here take for granted for the purpose of showing a thought which
has struck me concerning it) I say '*Soul making*' Soul as distinguished
from an Intelligence—There may be intelligences or sparks of the
divinity in millions—but they are not souls ~~the~~ till they acquire
identities, till each one is personally itself. I[n]telligences are atoms
of perception—they know and they see and they are pure, in short
they are God—how then are Souls to be made? How then are these
sparks which are God to have identity given them—so as ever to
possess a bliss peculiar to each ones individual existence? How, but
by the medium of a world like this? This point I sincerely wish to
consider because I think it a grander system of salvation than the
chrystain religion—or rather it is a system of Spirit-creation—This
is effected by three grand materials acting the one upon the other
for a series of years—These three Materials are the *Intelligence*—the
human heart (as distinguished from intelligence or Mind) and the
World or *Elemental space* suited for the proper action of *Mind and
Heart* on each other for the purpose of forming the *Soul* or *Intel-
ligence destined to possess the sense of Identity*. I can scarcely express
what I but dimly perceive—and yet I think I perceive it—that you
may judge the more clearly I will put it in the most homely form
possible—I will call the *world* a School instituted for the purpose of
teaching little children to read—I will call the *human heart* the *horn
Book* used in that School—and I will call the *Child able to read, the*

117

Soul made from that *school* and its *hornbook*. Do you not see how necessary a World of Pains and troubles is to school an Intelligence and make it a soul? A Place where the heart must feel and suffer in a thousand diverse ways! Not merely is the Heart a Hornbook, It is the Minds Bible, it is the Minds experience, it is the teat from which the Mind or intelligence sucks its identity—As various as the Lives of Men are—so various become their Souls, and thus does God make individual beings, Souls, Identical Souls of the sparks of his own essence—This appears to me a faint sketch of a system of Salvation which does not affront our reason and humanity—I am convinced that many difficulties which christians labour under would vanish before it—There is one wh[i]ch even now Strikes me —the Salvation of Children—In them the Spark or intelligence returns to God without any identity—it having had no time to learn of, and be altered by, the heart—or seat of the human Passions —It is pretty generally suspected that the chr[i]stian scheme has been coppied from the ancient persian and greek Philosophers. Why may they not have made this simple thing even more simple for common apprehension by introducing Mediators and Personages in the same manner as in the he[a]then mythology abstractions are personified— Seriously I think it probable that this System of Soul-making—may have been the Parent of all the more palpable and personal Schemes of Redemption, among the Zoroastrians the Christians and the Hindoos. For as one part of the human species must have their carved Jupiter; so another part must have the palpable and named Mediatior and saviour, their Christ their Oromanes and their Vishnu —If what I have said should not be plain enough, as I fear it may not be, I will but [*for* put] you in the place where I began in this series of thoughts—I mean, I began by seeing how man was formed by circumstances—and what are circumstances?—but touchstones of his heart—? and what are touchstones? but proovings of his heart?—and what are proovings of his heart but fortifiers or alterers of his nature? and what is his altered nature but his soul?—and what was his soul before it came into the world and had These provings and alterations and perfectionings?—An intelligence—without

Identity—and how is this Identity to be made? Through the medium of the Heart? And how is the heart to become this Medium but in a world of Circumstances?—There now I think what with Poetry and Theology you may thank your Stars that my pen is not very long winded. . . .

Ode to Psyche

O GODDESS! hear these tuneless numbers, wrung
    By sweet enforcement and remembrance dear,
And pardon that thy secrets should be sung
    Even into thine own soft-conchèd ear:
Surely I dreamt to-day, or did I see
    The wingèd Psyche with awaken'd eyes?
I wander'd in a forest thoughtlessly,
    And, on the sudden, fainting with surprise,
Saw two fair creatures, couchèd side by side
    In deepest grass, beneath the whisp'ring roof   10
Of leaves and trembled blossoms, where there ran
      A brooklet, scarce espied:
'Mid hush'd, cool-rooted flowers, fragrant-eyed,
    Blue, silver-white, and budded Tyrian,
They lay calm-breathing on the bedded grass;
    Their arms embracèd, and their pinions too;
    Their lips touch'd not, but had not bid adieu,
As if disjoined by soft-handed slumber,
And ready still past kisses to outnumber
    At tender eye-dawn of aurorean love: 20
      The wingèd boy I knew;
But who wast thou, O happy, happy dove?
      His Psyche true!

O latest born and loveliest vision far
  Of all Olympus' faded hierarchy!
Fairer than Phoebe's sapphire-region'd star,
  Or Vesper, amorous glow-worm of the sky;
Fairer than these, though temple thou hast none,
  Nor altar heap'd with flowers;
Nor virgin-choir to make delicious moan   30
  Upon the midnight hours;
No voice, no lute, no pipe, no incense sweet
  From chain-swung censer teeming;
No shrine, no grove, no oracle, no heat
  Of pale-mouth'd prophet dreaming.

O brightest! though too late for antique vows,
  Too, too late for the fond believing lyre,
When holy were the haunted forest boughs,
  Holy the air, the water, and the fire;
Yet even in these days so far retir'd   40
  From happy pieties, thy lucent fans,
  Fluttering among the faint Olympians,
I see, and sing, by my own eyes inspired.
So let me by thy choir, and make a moan
  Upon the midnight hours;
Thy voice, thy lute, thy pipe, thy incense sweet
  From swinged censer teeming;
Thy shrine, thy grove, thy oracle, thy heat
  Of pale-mouth'd prophet dreaming.

Yes, I will be thy priest, and build a fane   50
  In some untrodden region of my mind,
Where branched thoughts, new grown with pleasant pain,
  Instead of pines shall murmur in the wind:
Far, far around shall those dark-cluster'd trees
  Fledge the wild-ridged mountains steep by steep;
And there by zephyrs, streams, and birds, and bees,

The moss-lain Dryads shall be lull'd to sleep;
And in the midst of this wide quietness
A rosy sanctuary will I dress
With the wreath'd trellis of a working brain,   60
   With buds, and bells, and stars without a name,
With all the gardener Fancy e'er could feign,
   Who breeding flowers, will never breed the same:
And there shall be for thee all soft delight
   That shadowy thought can win,
A bright torch, and a casement ope at night,
   To let the warm Love in!

Ode on Indolence

'They toil not, neither do they spin.'

ONE morn before me were three figures seen,
With bowed necks, and joined hands, side-faced;
And one behind the other stepp'd serene,
In placid sandals, and in white robes graced;
They pass'd, like figures on a marble urn,
When shifted round to see the other side;
They came again; as when the urn once more
Is shifted round, the first seen shades return;
And they were strange to me, as may betide
With vases, to one deep in Phidian lore.   10

How is it, Shadows! that I knew ye not?
How came ye muffled in so hush a masque?
Was it a silent deep-disguised plot
To steal away, and leave without a task
My idle days? Ripe was the drowsy hour;
The blissful cloud of summer-indolence

Benumb'd my eyes; my pulse grew less and less;
Pain had no sting, and pleasure's wreath no flower:
O, why did ye not melt, and leave my sense
Unhaunted quite of all but—nothingness?   20

A third time came they by;—alas! wherefore?
My sleep had been embroider'd with dim dreams;
My soul had been a lawn besprinkled o'er
With flowers, and stirring shades, and baffled beams:
The morn was clouded, but no shower fell,
Tho' in her lids hung the sweet tears of May;
The open casement press'd a new-leav'd vine,
Let in the budding warmth and throstle's lay;
O Shadows! 'twas a time to bid farewell!
Upon your skirts had fallen no tears of mine.   30

A third time pass'd they by, and, passing, turn'd
Each one the face a moment whiles to me;
Then faded, and to follow them I burn'd
And ached for wings because I knew the three;
The first was a fair Maid, and Love her name;
The second was Ambition, pale of cheek,
And ever watchful with fatigued eye;
The last, whom I love more, the more of blame
Is heap'd upon her, maiden most unmeek,—
I knew to be my demon Poesy.   40

They faded, and, forsooth! I wanted wings:
O folly! What is Love! and where is it?
And for that poor Ambition—it springs
From a man's little heart's short fever-fit;
For Poesy!—no,—she has not a joy,—
At least for me,—so sweet as drowsy noons,
And evenings steep'd in honied indolence;
O, for an age so shelter'd from annoy,
That I may never know how change the moons,
Or hear the voice of busy common-sense!   50

So, ye three Ghosts, adieu! Ye cannot raise
My head cool-bedded in the flowery grass;
For I would not be dieted with praise,
A pet-lamb in a sentimental farce!
Fade softly from my eyes, and be once more
In masque-like figures on the dreamy urn;
Farewell! I yet have visions for the night,
And for the day faint visions there is store;
Vanish, ye Phantoms! from my idle spright,
Into the clouds, and never more return!   60

To FANNY KEATS
Saturday [*1 May 1819*]

                      Wentworth Place Saturday—
My dear Fanny,

    If it were but six oClock in the morning I would set off to see
you today: if I should so so now I could not stop long enough for a
how d'ye do—it is so long a walk through Hornsey and Tottenham
—and as for Stage Coaching it besides that it is very expensive it
is like going into the Boxes by way of the pit—I cannot go out on
Sunday—but if on Monday it should promise as fair as to day I
will put on a pair of loose easy palatable boots and me rendre chez
vous—I continue increasing my letter to George to send it by one
of Birkbeck's sons who is going out soon—so if you will let me
have a few more lines, they will be in time—I am glad you got on
so well with Monsr. le Curè—is he a nice Clergyman—a great deal
depends upon a cock'd hat and powder—not gun powder, lord love
us, but lady-meal, violet-smooth, dainty-scented lilly-white, feather-
soft, wigsby-dressing, coat-collar-spoiling whisker-reaching, pig-
tail loving, swans down-puffing, parson-sweetening powder—I
shall call in passing at the tottenham nursery and see if I can find
some seasonable plants for you. That is the nearest place—or by our
la'kin or lady kin, that is by the virgin Mary's kindred, is there not
a twig-manufacturer in Walthamstow? M^r & Mrs Dilke are coming

to dine with us to day—they will enjoy the country after West-
minster—O there is nothing like fine weather, and health, and
Books, and a fine country, and a contented Mind, and Diligent
habit of reading and thinking, and an amulet against the ennui—
and, please heaven, a little claret-wine cool out of a cellar a mile
deep—with a few or a good many ratafia cakes—a rocky basin to
bathe in, a strawberry bed to say your prayers to Flora in, a pad
nag to go you ten miles or so; two or three sensible people to chat
with; two or th[r]ee spiteful folkes to spar with; two or three odd
fishes to laugh at and two or three numskuls to argue with—instead
of using dumb bells on a rainy day— . . .

Ode to a Nightingale

I

MY heart aches, and a drowsy numbness pains
    My sense, as though of hemlock I had drunk,
Or emptied some dull opiate to the drains
    One minute past, and Lethe-wards had sunk:
'Tis not through envy of thy happy lot,
    But being too happy in thine happiness,—
        That thou, light-winged Dryad of the trees,
            In some melodious plot
Of beechen green, and shadows numberless,
    Singest of summer in full-throated ease.   10

2

O, for a draught of vintage! that hath been
    Cool'd a long age in the deep-delved earth,
Tasting of Flora and the country green,
    Dance, and Provençal song, and sunburnt mirth!
O for a beaker full of the warm South,

Full of the true, the blushful Hippocrene,
  With beaded bubbles winking at the brim,
    And purple-stained mouth;
That I might drink, and leave the world unseen,
And with thee fade away into the forest dim: 20

3

Fade far away, dissolve, and quite forget
  What thou among the leaves hast never known,
The weariness, the fever, and the fret
  Here, where men sit and hear each other groan;
Where palsy shakes a few, sad, last gray hairs,
    Where youth grows pale, and spectre-thin, and dies;
      Where but to think is to be full of sorrow
        And leaden-eyed despairs,
    Where Beauty cannot keep her lustrous eyes,
      Or new Love pine at them beyond to-morrow.   30

4

Away! away! for I will fly to thee,
  Not charioted by Bacchus and his pards,
But on the viewless wings of Poesy,
  Though the dull brain perplexes and retards:
Already with thee! tender is the night,
    And haply the Queen-Moon is on her throne,
      Cluster'd around by all her starry Fays;
        But here there is no light,
    Save what from heaven is with the breezes blown
      Through verdurous glooms and winding mossy ways.   40

5

I cannot see what flowers are at my feet,
  Nor what soft incense hangs upon the boughs,
But, in embalmed darkness, guess each sweet
  Wherewith the seasonable month endows

125

The grass, the thicket, and the fruit-tree wild;
   White hawthorn, and the pastoral eglantine;
     Fast fading violets cover'd up in leaves;
      And mid-May's eldest child,
The coming musk-rose, full of dewy wine,
   The murmurous haunt of flies on summer eves.   50

6

Darkling I listen; and, for many a time
   I have been half in love with easeful Death,
Call'd him soft names in many a mused rhyme,
   To take into the air my quiet breath;
Now more than ever seems it rich to die,
   To cease upon the midnight with no pain,
     While thou art pouring forth thy soul abroad
      In such an ecstasy!
Still wouldst thou sing, and I have ears in vain—
   To thy high requiem become a sod.   60

7

Thou wast not born for death, immortal Bird!
   No hungry generations tread thee down;
The voice I hear this passing night was heard
   In ancient days by emperor and clown:
Perhaps the self-same song that found a path
   Through the sad heart of Ruth, when, sick for home,
     She stood in tears amid the alien corn;
      The same that oft-times hath
Charm'd magic casements, opening on the foam
   Of perilous seas, in faery lands forlorn.   70

8

Forlorn! the very word is like a bell
   To toll me back from thee to my sole self!
Adieu! the fancy cannot cheat so well
   As she is fam'd to do, deceiving elf.

Adieu! adieu! thy plaintive anthem fades
    Past the near meadows, over the still stream,
        Up the hill-side; and now 'tis buried deep
            In the next valley-glades:
    Was it a vision, or a waking dream?
        Fled is that music:—Do I wake or sleep?   80

Ode on a Grecian Urn

1

THOU still unravish'd bride of quietness,
    Thou foster-child of silence and slow time,
Sylvan historian, who canst thus express
    A flowery tale more sweetly than our rhyme:
What leaf-fring'd legend haunts about thy shape
    Of deities or mortals, or of both,
        In Tempe or the dales of Arcady?
What men or gods are these? What maidens loth?
    What mad pursuit? What struggle to escape?
        What pipes and timbrels? What wild ecstasy?   10

2

Heard melodies are sweet, but those unheard
    Are sweeter; therefore, ye soft pipes, play on;
Not to the sensual ear, but, more endear'd,
    Pipe to the spirit ditties of no tone:
Fair youth, beneath the trees, thou canst not leave
    Thy song, nor ever can those trees be bare;
        Bold Lover, never, never canst thou kiss,
Though winning near the goal—yet, do not grieve;
    She cannot fade, though thou hast not thy bliss,
        For ever wilt thou love, and she be fair!   20

127

3

Ah, happy, happy boughs! that cannot shed
  Your leaves, nor ever bid the Spring adieu;
And, happy melodist, unwearied,
  For ever piping songs for ever new;
More happy love! more happy, happy love!
  For ever warm and still to be enjoy'd,
    For ever panting, and for ever young;
All breathing human passion far above,
  That leaves a heart high-sorrowful and cloy'd,
    A burning forehead, and a parching tongue.   30

4

Who are these coming to the sacrifice?
  To what green altar, O mysterious priest,
Lead'st thou that heifer lowing at the skies,
  And all her silken flanks with garlands drest?
What little town by river or sea shore,
  Or mountain-built with peaceful citadel,
    Is emptied of this folk, this pious morn?
And, little town, thy streets for evermore
  Will silent be; and not a soul to tell
    Why thou art desolate, can e'er return.   40

5

O Attic shape! Fair attitude! with brede
  Of marble men and maidens overwrought,
With forest branches and the trodden weed;
  Thou, silent form, dost tease us out of thought
As doth eternity: Cold Pastoral!
  When old age shall this generation waste,
    Thou shalt remain, in midst of other woe
Than ours, a friend to man, to whom thou say'st,
  Beauty is truth, truth beauty,—that is all
    Ye know on earth, and all ye need to know.   50

Ode on Melancholy

1

No, no, go not to Lethe, neither twist
  Wolf's-bane, tight-rooted, for its poisonous wine;
Nor suffer thy pale forehead to be kiss'd
  By nightshade, ruby grape of Proserpine;
Make not your rosary of yew-berries,
  Nor let the beetle, nor the death-moth be
    Your mournful Psyche, nor the downy owl
A partner in your sorrow's mysteries;
  For shade to shade will come too drowsily,
    And drown the wakeful anguish of the soul.   10

2

But when the melancholy fit shall fall
  Sudden from heaven like a weeping cloud,
That fosters the droop-headed flowers all,
  And hides the green hill in an April shroud;
Then glut thy sorrow on a morning rose,
  Or on the rainbow of the salt sand-wave,
    Or on the wealth of globed peonies;
Or if thy mistress some rich anger shows,
  Emprison her soft hand, and let her rave,
    And feed deep, deep upon her peerless eyes.   20

3

She dwells with Beauty—Beauty that must die;
  And Joy, whose hand is ever at his lips
Bidding adieu; and aching Pleasure nigh,
  Turning to poison while the bee-mouth sips:
Ay, in the very temple of Delight

129

Veil'd Melancholy has her sovran shrine,
    Though seen of none save him whose strenuous tongue
Can burst Joy's grape against his palate fine;
    His soul shall taste the sadness of her might,
        And be among her cloudy trophies hung.   30

Lamia

PART I

UPON a time, before the faery broods
Drove Nymph and Satyr from the prosperous woods,
Before King Oberon's bright diadem,
Sceptre, and mantle, clasp'd with dewy gem,
Frighted away the Dryads and the Fauns
From rushes green, and brakes, and cowslip'd lawns,
The ever-smitten Hermes empty left
His golden throne, bent warm on amorous theft:
From high Olympus had he stolen light,
On this side of Jove's clouds, to escape the sight   10
Of his great summoner, and made retreat
Into a forest on the shores of Crete.
For somewhere in that sacred island dwelt
A nymph, to whom all hoofed Satyrs knelt;
At whose white feet the languid Tritons poured
Pearls, while on land they wither'd and adored.
Fast by the springs where she to bathe was wont,
And in those meads where sometime she might haunt,
Were strewn rich gifts, unknown to any Muse,
Though Fancy's casket were unlock'd to choose.   20
Ah, what a world of love was at her feet!
So Hermes thought, and a celestial heat
Burnt from his winged heels to either ear,

That from a whiteness, as the lily clear,
Blush'd into roses 'mid his golden hair,
Fallen in jealous curls about his shoulders bare.
From vale to vale, from wood to wood, he flew,
Breathing upon the flowers his passion new,
And wound with many a river to its head,
To find where this sweet nymph prepar'd her secret bed: 30
In vain; the sweet nymph might nowhere be found,
And so he rested, on the lonely ground,
Pensive, and full of painful jealousies
Of the Wood-Gods, and even the very trees.
There as he stood, he heard a mournful voice,
Such as once heard, in gentle heart, destroys
All pain but pity: thus the lone voice spake:
'When from this wreathed tomb shall I awake!
'When move in a sweet body fit for life,
'And love, and pleasure, and the ruddy strife   40
'Of hearts and lips! Ah, miserable me!
The God, dove-footed, glided silently
Round bush and tree, soft-brushing, in his speed,
The taller grasses and full-flowering weed,
Until he found a palpitating snake,
Bright, and cirque-couchant in a dusky brake.

She was a gordian shape of dazzling hue,
Vermilion-spotted, golden, green, and blue;
Striped like a zebra, freckled like a pard,
Eyed like a peacock, and all crimson barr'd;   50
And full of silver moons, that, as she breathed,
Dissolv'd, or brighter shone, or interwreathed
Their lustres with the gloomier tapestries—
So rainbow-sided, touch'd with miseries,
She seem'd, at once, some penanced lady elf,
Some demon's mistress, or the demon's self.
Upon her crest she wore a wannish fire

131

Sprinkled with stars, like Ariadne's tiar:
Her head was serpent, but ah, bitter-sweet!
She had a woman's mouth with all its pearls complete:　60
And for her eyes: what could such eyes do there
But weep, and weep, that they were born so fair?
As Proserpine still weeps for her Sicilian air.
Her throat was serpent, but the words she spake
Came, as through bubbling honey, for Love's sake,
And thus; while Hermes on his pinions lay,
Like a stoop'd falcon ere he takes his prey.

'Fair Hermes, crown'd with feathers, fluttering light,
'I had a splendid dream of thee last night:
'I saw thee sitting, on a throne of gold,　70
'Among the Gods, upon Olympus old,
'The only sad one; for thou didst not hear
'The soft, lute-finger'd Muses chaunting clear,
'Nor even Apollo when he sang alone,
'Deaf to his throbbing throat's long, long melodious moan.
'I dreamt I saw thee, robed in purple flakes,
'Break amorous through the clouds, as morning breaks,
'And, swiftly as a bright Phoebean dart,
'Strike for the Cretan isle; and here thou art!
'Too gentle Hermes, hast thou found the maid?'　80
Whereat the star of Lethe not delay'd
His rosy eloquence, and thus inquired:
'Thou smooth-lipp'd serpent, surely high inspired!
'Thou beauteous wreath, with melancholy eyes,
'Possess whatever bliss thou canst devise,
'Telling me only where my nymph is fled,—
'Where she doth breathe!' 'Bright planet, thou hast said,'
Return'd the snake, 'but seal with oaths, fair God!'
'I swear,' said Hermes, 'by my serpent rod,
'And by thine eyes, and by thy starry crown!'　90
Light flew his earnest words, among the blossoms blown.

Then thus again the brilliance feminine:
'Too frail of heart! for this lost nymph of thine,
'Free as the air, invisibly, she strays
'About these thornless wilds; her pleasant days
'She tastes unseen; unseen her nimble feet
'Leave traces in the grass and flowers sweet;
'From weary tendrils, and bow'd branches green,
'She plucks the fruit unseen, she bathes unseen:
'And by my power is her beauty veil'd   100
'To keep it unaffronted, unassail'd
'By the love-glances of unlovely eyes,
'Of Satyrs, Fauns, and blear'd Silenus' sighs.
'Pale grew her immortality, for woe
'Of all these lovers, and she grieved so
'I took compassion on her, bade her steep
'Her hair in weïrd syrops, that would keep
'Her loveliness invisible, yet free
'To wander as she loves, in liberty.
'Thou shalt behold her, Hermes, thou alone,   110
'If thou wilt, as thou swearest, grant my boon!'
Then, once again, the charmed God began
An oath, and through the serpent's ears it ran
Warm, tremulous, devout, psalterian.
Ravish'd, she lifted her Circean head,
Blush'd a live damask, and swift-lisping said,
'I was a woman, let me have once more
'A woman's shape, and charming as before.
'I love a youth of Corinth—O the bliss!
'Give me my woman's form, and place me where he is.   120
'Stoop, Hermes, let me breathe upon thy brow,
'And thou shalt see thy sweet nymph even now.'
The God on half-shut feathers sank serene,
She breath'd upon his eyes, and swift was seen
Of both the guarded nymph near-smiling on the green.
It was no dream; or say a dream it was,

Real are the dreams of Gods, and smoothly pass
Their pleasures in a long immortal dream.
One warm, flush'd moment, hovering, it might seem
Dashed by the wood-nymph's beauty, so he burn'd;   130
Then, lighting on the printless verdure, turn'd
To the swoon'd serpent, and with languid arm,
Delicate, put to proof the lythe Caducean charm.
So done, upon the nymph his eyes he bent
Full of adoring tears and blandishment,
And towards her stept: she, like a moon in wane,
Faded before him, cower'd, nor could restrain
Her fearful sobs, self-folding like a flower
That faints into itself at evening hour:
But the God fostering her chilled hand,   140
She felt the warmth, her eyelids open'd bland,
And, like new flowers at morning song of bees,
Bloom'd, and gave up her honey to the lees.
Into the green-recessed woods they flew;
Nor grew they pale, as mortal lovers do.

    Left to herself, the serpent now began
To change; her elfin blood in madness ran,
Her mouth foam'd, and the grass, therewith besprent,
Wither'd at dew so sweet and virulent;
Her eyes in torture fix'd, and anguish drear,   150
Hot, glaz'd, and wide, with lid-lashes all sear,
Flash'd phosphor and sharp sparks, without one cooling tear.
The colours all inflam'd throughout her train,
She writh'd about, convuls'd with scarlet pain:
A deep volcanian yellow took the place
Of all her milder-mooned body's grace;
And, as the lava ravishes the mead,
Spoilt all her silver mail, and golden brede,
Made gloom of all her frecklings, streaks and bars,
Eclips'd her crescents, and lick'd up her stars: 160

So that, in moments few, she was undrest
Of all her sapphires, greens, and amethyst,
And rubious-argent: of all these bereft,
Nothing but pain and ugliness were left.
Still shone her crown; that vanish'd, also she
Melted and disappear'd as suddenly;
And in the air, her new voice luting soft,
Cried, 'Lycius! gentle Lycius!'—Borne aloft
With the bright mists about the mountains hoar
These words dissolv'd: Crete's forests heard no more.   170

  Whither fled Lamia, now a lady bright,
A full-born beauty new and exquisite?
She fled into that valley they pass o'er
Who go to Corinth from Cenchreas' shore;
And rested at the foot of those wild hills,
The rugged founts of the Peraean rills,
And of that other ridge whose barren back
Stretches, with all its mist and cloudy rack,
South-westward to Cleone. There she stood
About a young bird's flutter from a wood,   180
Fair, on a sloping green of mossy tread,
By a clear pool, wherein she passioned
To see herself escap'd from so sore ills,
While her robes flaunted with the daffodils.

  Ah, happy Lycius!—for she was a maid
More beautiful than ever twisted braid,
Or sigh'd, or blush'd, or on spring-flowered lea
Spread a green kirtle to the minstrelsy:
A virgin purest lipp'd, yet in the lore
Of love deep learned to the red heart's core: 190
Not one hour old, yet of sciential brain
To unperplex bliss from its neighbour pain;

135

Define their pettish limits, and estrange
Their points of contact, and swift counterchange;
Intrigue with the specious chaos, and dispart
Its most ambiguous atoms with sure art;
As though in Cupid's college she had spent
Sweet days a lovely graduate, still unshent,
And kept his rosy terms in idle languishment.

Why this fair creature chose so fairily   200
By the wayside to linger, we shall see;
But first 'tis fit to tell how she could muse
And dream, when in the serpent prison-house,
Of all she list, strange or magnificent:
How, ever, where she will'd, her spirit went;
Whether to faint Elysium, or where
Down through tress-lifting waves the Nereids fair
Wind into Thetis' bower by many a pearly stair;
Or where God Bacchus drains his cups divine,
Stretch'd out, at ease, beneath a glutinous pine;   210
Or where in Pluto's gardens palatine
Mulciber's columns gleam in far piazzian line.
And sometimes into cities she would send
Her dream, with feast and rioting to blend;
And once, while among mortals dreaming thus,
She saw the young Corinthian Lycius
Charioting foremost in the envious race,
Like a young Jove with calm uneager face,
And fell into a swooning love of him.
Now on the moth-time of that evening dim   220
He would return that way, as well she knew,
To Corinth from the shore; for freshly blew
The eastern soft wind, and his galley now
Grated the quaystones with her brazen prow
In port Cenchreas, from Egina isle
Fresh anchor'd; whether he had been awhile

To sacrifice to Jove, whose temple there
Waits with high marble doors for blood and incense rare.
Jove heard his vows, and better'd his desire;
For by some freakful chance he made retire   230
From his companions, and set forth to walk,
Perhaps grown wearied of their Corinth talk:
Over the solitary hills he fared,
Thoughtless at first, but ere eve's star appeared
His phantasy was lost, where reason fades,
In the calm'd twilight of Platonic shades.
Lamia beheld him coming, near, more near—
Close to her passing, in indifference drear,
His silent sandals swept the mossy green;
So neighbour'd to him, and yet so unseen   240
She stood: he pass'd, shut up in mysteries,
His mind wrapp'd like his mantle, while her eyes
Follow'd his steps, and her neck regal white
Turn'd—syllabling thus, 'Ah, Lycius bright,
'And will you leave me on the hills alone?
'Lycius, look back! and be some pity shown.'
He did; not with cold wonder fearingly,
But Orpheus-like at an Eurydice;
For so delicious were the words she sung,
It seem'd he had loved them a whole summer long: 250
And soon his eyes had drunk her beauty up,
Leaving no drop in the bewildering cup,
And still the cup was full,—while he, afraid
Lest she should vanish ere his lip had paid
Due adoration, thus began to adore;
Her soft look growing coy, she saw his chain so sure:
'Leave thee alone! Look back! Ah, Goddess, see
'Whether my eyes can ever turn from thee!
'For pity do not this sad heart belie—
'Even as thou vanishest so I shall die.   260
'Stay! though a Naiad of the rivers, stay!

'To thy far wishes will thy streams obey:
'Stay! though the greenest woods be thy domain,
'Alone they can drink up the morning rain:
'Though a descended Pleiad, will not one
'Of thine harmonious sisters keep in tune
'Thy spheres, and as thy silver proxy shine?
'So sweetly to these ravish'd ears of mine
'Came thy sweet greeting, that if thou shouldst fade
'Thy memory will waste me to a shade:—   270
'For pity do not melt!'—'If I should stay,'
Said Lamia, 'here, upon this floor of clay,
'And pain my steps upon these flowers too rough,
'What canst thou say or do of charm enough
'To dull the nice remembrance of my home?
'Thou canst not ask me with thee here to roam
'Over these hills and vales, where no joy is,—
'Empty of immortality and bliss!
'Thou art a scholar, Lycius, and must know
'That finer spirits cannot breathe below   280
'In human climes, and live: Alas! poor youth,
'What taste of purer air hast thou to soothe
'My essence? What serener palaces,
'Where I may all my many senses please,
'And by mysterious sleights a hundred thirsts appease?
'It cannot be—Adieu!' So said, she rose
Tiptoe with white arms spread. He, sick to lose
The amorous promise of her lone complain,
Swoon'd, murmuring of love, and pale with pain.
The cruel lady, without any show   290
Of sorrow for her tender favourite's woe,
But rather, if her eyes could brighter be,
With brighter eyes and slow amenity,
Put her new lips to his, and gave afresh
The life she had so tangled in her mesh:
And as he from one trance was wakening

Into another, she began to sing,
Happy in beauty, life, and love, and every thing,
A song of love, too sweet for earthly lyres,
While, like held breath, the stars drew in their panting fires.
And then she whisper'd in such trembling tone,   301
As those who, safe together met alone
For the first time through many anguish'd days,
Use other speech than looks; bidding him raise
His drooping head, and clear his soul of doubt,
For that she was a woman, and without
Any more subtle fluid in her veins
Than throbbing blood, and that the self-same pains
Inhabited her frail-strung heart as his.
And next she wonder'd how his eyes could miss   310
Her face so long in Corinth, where, she said,
She dwelt but half retir'd, and there had led
Days happy as the gold coin could invent
Without the aid of love; yet in content
Till she saw him, as once she pass'd him by,
Where 'gainst a column he leant thoughtfully
At Venus' temple porch, 'mid baskets heap'd
Of amorous herbs and flowers, newly reap'd
Late on that eve, as 'twas the night before
The Adonian feast; whereof she saw no more,   320
But wept alone those days, for why should she adore?
Lycius from death awoke into amaze,
To see her still, and singing so sweet lays;
Then from amaze into delight he fell
To hear her whisper woman's lore so well;
And every word she spake entic'd him on
To unperplex'd delight and pleasure known.
Let the mad poets say whate'er they please
Of the sweets of Fairies, Peris, Goddesses,
There is not such a treat among them all,   330
Haunters of cavern, lake, and waterfall,

139

As a real woman, lineal indeed
From Pyrrha's pebbles or old Adam's seed.
Thus gentle Lamia judg'd, and judg'd aright,
That Lycius could not love in half a fright,
So threw the goddess off, and won his heart
More pleasantly by playing woman's part,
With no more awe than what her beauty gave,
That, while it smote, still guaranteed to save.
Lycius to all made eloquent reply,   340
Marrying to every word a twinborn sigh;
And last, pointing to Corinth, ask'd her sweet,
If 'twas too far that night for her soft feet.
The way was short, for Lamia's eagerness
Made, by a spell, the triple league decrease
To a few paces; not at all surmised
By blinded Lycius, so in her comprized.
They pass'd the city gates, he knew not how,
So noiseless, and he never thought to know.

As men talk in a dream, so Corinth all,   350
Throughout her palaces imperial,
And all her populous streets and temples lewd,
Mutter'd, like tempest in the distance brew'd,
To the wide-spreaded night above her towers.
Men, women, rich and poor, in the cool hours,
Shuffled their sandals o'er the pavement white,
Companion'd or alone; while many a light
Flared, here and there, from wealthy festivals,
And threw their moving shadows on the walls,
Or found them cluster'd in the corniced shade   360
Of some arch'd temple door, or dusky colonnade.

Muffling his face, of greeting friends in fear,
Her fingers he press'd hard, as one came near

With curl'd gray beard, sharp eyes, and smooth bald crown,
Slow-stepp'd, and robed in philosophic gown:
Lycius shrank closer, as they met and past,
Into his mantle, adding wings to haste,
While hurried Lamia trembled: 'Ah,' said he,
'Why do you shudder, love, so ruefully?
'Why does your tender palm dissolve in dew?'—   370
I'm wearied,' said fair Lamia: 'tell me who
'Is that old man? I cannot bring to mind
'His features:—Lycius! wherefore did you blind
'Yourself from his quick eyes?' Lycius replied,
''Tis Apollonius sage, my trusty guide
'And good instructor; but to-night he seems
'The ghost of folly haunting my sweet dreams.'

    While yet he spake they had arrived before
A pillar'd porch, with lofty portal door,
Where hung a silver lamp, whose phosphor glow   380
Reflected in the slabbed steps below,
Mild as a star in water; for so new,
And so unsullied was the marble hue,
So through the crystal polish, liquid fine,
Ran the dark veins, that none but feet divine
Could e'er have touch'd there. Sounds Æolian
Breath'd from the hinges, as the ample span
Of the wide doors disclos'd a place unknown
Sometime to any, but those two alone,
And a few Persian mutes, who that same year   390
Were seen about the markets: none knew where
They could inhabit; the most curious
Were foil'd, who watch'd to trace them to their house:
And but the flitter-winged verse must tell
For truth's sake, what woe afterwards befel,
'Twould humour many a heart to leave them thus,
Shut from the busy world of more incredulous.

LOVE in a hut, with water and a crust,
Is—Love, forgive us!—cinders, ashes, dust;
Love in a palace is perhaps at last
More grievious torment than a hermit's fast:—
That is a doubtful tale from faery land,
Hard for the non-elect to understand.
Had Lycius liv'd to hand his story down,
He might have given the moral a fresh frown,
Or clench'd it quite: but too short was their bliss
To breed distrust and hate, that make the soft voice hiss.   10
Besides, there, nightly, with terrific glare,
Love, jealous grown of so complete a pair,
Hover'd and buzz'd his wings, with fearful roar,
Above the lintel of their chamber door,
And down the passage cast a glow upon the floor.

    For all this came a ruin: side by side
They were enthroned, in the even tide,
Upon a couch, near to a curtaining
Whose airy texture, from a golden string,
Floated into the room, and let appear   20
Unveil'd, the summer heaven, blue and clear,
Betwixt two marble shafts:—there they reposed,
Where use had made it sweet, with eyelids closed,
Saving a tythe which love still open kept,
That they might see each other while they almost slept;
When from the slope side of a suburb hill,
Deafening the swallow's twitter, came a thrill
Of trumpets—Lycius started—the sounds fled,
But left a thought a-buzzing in his head.
For the first time, since first he harbour'd in   30

That purple-lined palace of sweet sin,
His spirit pass'd beyond its golden bourn
Into the noisy world almost forsworn.
The lady, every watchful, penetrant,
Saw this with pain, so arguing a want
Of something more, more than her empery
Of joys; and she began to moan and sigh
Because he mused beyond her, knowing well
That but a moment's thought is passion's passing bell.
'Why do you sigh, fair creature?' whisper'd he: 40
'Why do you think?' return'd she tenderly:
'You have deserted me;—where am I now?
'Not in your heart while care weighs on your brow:
'No, no, you have dismiss'd me; and I go
'From your breast houseless: ay, it must be so.'
He answer'd, bending to her open eyes,
Where he was mirror'd small in paradise,
'My silver planet, both of eve and morn!
'Why will you plead yourself so sad forlorn,
'While I am striving how to fill my heart   50
'With deeper crimson, and a double smart?
'How to entangle, trammel up and snare
'Your soul in mine, and labyrinth you there
'Like the hid scent in an unbudded rose?
'Ay, a sweet kiss—you see your mighty woes.
'My thoughts! shall I unveil them? Listen then!
'What mortal hath a prize, that other men
'May be confounded and abash'd withal,
'But lets it sometimes pace abroad majestical,
'And triumph, as in thee I should rejoice   60
'Amid the hoarse alarm of Corinth's voice.
'Let my foes choke, and my friends shout afar,
'While through the throned streets your bridal car
'Wheels round its dazzling spokes.'—The lady's cheek
Trembled; she nothing said, but, pale and meek,

143

Arose and knelt before him, wept a rain
Of sorrows at his words; at last with pain
Beseeching him, the while his hand she wrung,
To change his purpose. He thereat was stung,
Perverse, with stronger fancy to reclaim   70
Her wild and timid nature to his aim:
Besides, for all his love, in self despite
Against his better self, he took delight
Luxurious in her sorrows, soft and new.
His passion, cruel grown, took on a hue
Fierce and sanguineous as 'twas possible
In one whose brow had no dark veins to swell.
Fine was the mitigated fury, like
Apollo's presence when in act to strike
The serpent—Ha, the serpent! certes, she   80
Was none. She burnt, she lov'd the tyranny,
And, all subdued, consented to the hour
When to the bridal he should lead his paramour.
Whispering in midnight silence, said the youth,
'Sure some sweet name thou hast, though, by my truth,
'I have not ask'd it, ever thinking thee
'Not mortal, but of heavenly progeny,
'As still I do. Hast any mortal name,
'Fit appellation for this dazzling frame?
'Or friends or kinsfolk on the cited earth,   90
'To share our marriage feast and nuptial mirth?'
'I have no friends,' said Lamia, 'no, not one;
'My presence in wide Corinth hardly known:
'My parents' bones are in their dusty urns
'Sepulchred, where no kindled incense burns,
'Seeing all their luckless race are dead, save me,
'And I neglect the holy rite for thee.
'Even as you list invite your many guests;
'But if, as now it seems, your vision rests
'With any pleasure on me, do not bid   100

144

'Old Apollonius—from him keep me hid.'
Lycius, perplex'd at words so blind and blank,
Made close inquiry; from whose touch she shrank,
Feigning a sleep; and he to the dull shade
Of deep sleep in a moment was betray'd.

It was the custom then to bring away
The bride from home at blushing shut of day,
Veil'd, in a chariot, heralded along
By strewn flowers, torches, and a marriage song,
With other pageants: but this fair unknown   110
Had not a friend. So being left alone,
(Lycius was gone to summon all his kin)
And knowing surely she could never win
His foolish heart from its mad pompousness,
She set herself, high-thoughted, how to dress
The misery in fit magnificence.
She did so, but 'tis doubtful how and whence
Came, and who were her subtle servitors.
About the halls, and to and from the doors,
There was a noise of wings, till in short space   120
The glowing banquet-room shone with wide-arched grace.
A haunting music, sole perhaps and lone
Supportress of the faery-roof, made moan
Throughout, as fearful the whole charm might fade.
Fresh carved cedar, mimicking a glade
Of palm and plantain, met from either side,
High in the midst, in honour of the bride:
Two palms and then two plantains, and so on,
From either side their stems branch'd one to one
All down the aisled place; and beneath all   130
There ran a stream of lamps straight on from wall to wall.
So canopied, lay an untasted feast
Teeming with odours. Lamia, regal drest,
Silently paced about, and as she went,

In pale contented sort of discontent,
Mission'd her viewless servants to enrich
The fretted splendour of each nook and niche.
Between the tree-stems, marbled plain at first,
Came jasper pannels; then, anon, there burst
Forth creeping imagery of slighter trees,   140
And with the larger wove in small intricacies.
Approving all, she faded at self-will,
And shut the chamber up, close, hush'd and still,
Complete and ready for the revels rude,
When dreadful guests would come to spoil her solitude.

    The day appear'd, and all the gossip rout.
O senseless Lycius! Madman! wherefore flout
The silent-blessing fate, warm cloister'd hours,
And show to common eyes these secret bowers?
The herd approach'd; each guest, with busy brain,   150
Arriving at the portal, gaz'd amain,
And enter'd marveling: for they knew the street,
Remember'd it from childhood all complete
Without a gap, yet ne'er before had seen
That royal porch, that high-built fair demesne;
So in they hurried all, maz'd, curious and keen:
Save one, who look'd thereon with eye severe,
And with calm-planted steps walk'd in austere;
'Twas Apollonius: something too he laugh'd,
As though some knotty problem, that had daft   160
His patient thought, had now begun to thaw,
And solve and melt:—'twas just as he foresaw.

    He met within the murmurous vestibule
His young disciple. "'Tis no common rule,
'Lycius,' said he, 'for uninvited guest
'To force himself upon you, and infest
'With an unbidden presence the bright throng
'Of younger friends; yet must I do this wrong,

'And you forgive me.' Lycius blush'd, and led
The old man through the inner doors broad-spread;   170
With reconciling words and courteous mien
Turning into sweet milk the sophist's spleen.

Of wealthy lustre was the banquet-room,
Fill'd with pervading brilliance and perfume:
Before each lucid pannel fuming stood
A censer fed with myrrh and spiced wood,
Each by a sacred tripod held aloft,
Whose slender feet wide-swerv'd upon the soft
Wool-woofed carpets: fifty wreaths of smoke
From fifty censers their light voyage took   180
To the high roof, still mimick'd as they rose
Along the mirror'd walls by twin-clouds odorous.
Twelve sphered tables, by silk seats insphered,
High as the level of a man's breast rear'd
On libbard's paws, upheld the heavy gold
Of cups and goblets, and the store thrice told
Of Ceres' horn, and, in huge vessels, wine
Come from the gloomy tun with merry shine.
Thus loaded with a feast the tables stood,
Each shrining in the midst the image of a God.   190

When in an antichamber every guest
Had felt the cold full sponge to pleasure press'd,
By minist'ring slaves, upon his hands and feet,
And fragrant oils with ceremony meet
Pour'd on his hair, they all mov'd to the feast
In white robes, and themselves in order placed
Around the silken couches, wondering
Whence all this mighty cost and blaze of wealth could spring.

Soft went the music the soft air along,
While fluent Greek a vowel'd undersong   200

147

Kept up among the guests, discoursing low
At first, for scarcely was the wine at flow;
But when the happy vintage touch'd their brains,
Louder they talk, and louder come the strains
Of powerful instruments:—the gorgeous dyes,
The space, the splendour of the draperies,
The roof of awful richness, nectarous cheer,
Beautiful slaves, and Lamia's self, appear,
Now, when the wine has done its rosy deed,
And every soul from human trammels freed,   210
No more so strange; for merry wine, sweet wine,
Will make Elysian shades not too fair, too divine.
Soon was God Bacchus at meridian height;
Flush'd were their cheeks, and bright eyes double bright:
Garlands of every green, and every scent
From vales deflower'd, or forest-trees branch-rent,
In baskets of bright osier'd gold were brought
High as the handles heap'd, to suit the thought
Of every guest; that each, as he did please,
Might fancy-fit his brows, silk-pillow'd at his ease.   220

What wreath for Lamia? What for Lycius?
What for the sage, old Apollonius?
Upon her aching forehead be there hung
The leaves of willow and of adder's tongue;
And for the youth, quick, let us strip for him
The thyrsus, that his watching eyes may swim
Into forgetfulness; and, for the sage,
Let spear-grass and the spiteful thistle wage
War on his temples. Do not all charms fly
At the mere touch of cold philosophy?   230
There was an awful rainbow once in heaven:
We know her woof, her texture; she is given
In the dull catalogue of common things.
Philosophy will clip an Angel's wings,

148

Conquer all mysteries by rule and line,
Empty the haunted air, and gnomed mine—
Unweave a rainbow, as it erewhile made
The tender-person'd Lamia melt into a shade.

By her glad Lycius sitting, in chief place,
Scarce saw in all the room another face,   240
Till, checking his love trance, a cup he took
Full brimm'd, and opposite sent forth a look
'Cross the broad table, to beseech a glance
From his old teacher's wrinkled countenance,
And pledge him. The bald-head philosopher
Had fix'd his eye, without a twinkle or stir
Full on the alarmed beauty of the bride,
Brow-beating her fair form, and troubling her sweet pride.
Lycius then press'd her hand, with devout touch,
As pale it lay upon the rosy couch: 250
'Twas icy, and the cold ran through his veins:
Then sudden it grew hot, and all the pains
Of an unnatural heat shot to his heart.
'Lamia, what means this? Wherefore dost thou start?
'Know'st thou that man?' Poor Lamia answer'd not.
He gaz'd into her eyes, and not a jot
Own'd they the lovelorn piteous appeal:
More, more he gaz'd: his human senses reel:
Some hungry spell that loveliness absorbs;
There was no recognition in those orbs.   260
'Lamia!' he cried—and no soft-toned reply.
The many heard, and the loud revelry
Grew hush; the stately music no more breathes;
The myrtle sicken'd in a thousand wreaths.
By faint degrees, voice, lute, and pleasure ceased;
A deadly silence step by step increased,
Until it seem'd a horrid presence there,
And not a man but felt the terror in his hair.

'Lamia!' he shriek'd; and nothing but the shriek
With its sad echo did the silence break.   270
'Begone, foul dream!' he cried, gazing again
In the bride's face, where now no azure vein
Wander'd on fair-spaced temples; no soft bloom
Misted the cheek; no passion to illume
The deep-recessed vision:—all was blight;
Lamia, no longer fair, there sat a deadly white.
'Shut, shut those juggling eyes, thou ruthless man!
'Turn them aside, wretch! or the righteous ban
'Of all the Gods, whose dreadful images
'Here represent their shadowy presences,   280
'May pierce them on the sudden with the thorn
'Of painful blindness; leaving thee forlorn,
'In trembling dotage to the feeblest fright
'Of conscience, for their long offended might,
'For all thine impious proud-heart sophistries,
'Unlawful magic, and enticing lies.
'Corinthians! look upon that gray-beard wretch!
'Mark how, possess'd, his lashless eyelids stretch
'Around his demon eyes! Corinthians, see!
'My sweet bride withers at their potency.'   290
'Fool!' said the sophist, in an under-tone
Gruff with contempt; which a death-nighing moan
From Lycius answer'd, as heart-struck and lost,
He sank supine beside the aching ghost.
'Fool! Fool!' repeated he, while his eyes still
Relented not, nor mov'd; 'from every ill
'Of life have I preserv'd thee to this day,
'And shall I see thee made a serpent's prey?'
Then Lamia breath'd death breath; the sophist's eye,
Like a sharp spear, went through her utterly,   300
Keen, cruel, perceant, stinging: she, as well
As her weak hand could any meaning tell,
Motion'd him to be silent; vainly so,

He look'd and look'd again a level—No!
'A Serpent!' echoed he; no sooner said,
Than with a frightful scream she vanished:
And Lycius' arms were empty of delight,
As were his limbs of life, from that same night,
On the high couch he lay!—his friends came round—
Supported him—no pulse, or breath they found,   310
And, in its marriage robe, the heavy body wound.

King Stephen

A Fragment of a Tragedy

ACT I

SCENE I. Field of Battle

Alarum. Enter KING STEPHEN, KNIGHTS, *and* SOLDIERS

STEPHEN: If shame can on a soldier's vein-swoll'n front
    Spread deeper crimson than the battle's toil,
    Blush in your casing helmets! for see, see!
    Yonder my chivalry, my pride of war,
    Wrench'd with an iron hand from firm array,
    Are routed loose about the plashy meads,
    Of honour forfeit. O that my known voice
    Could reach your dastard ears, and fright you more!
    Fly, cowards, fly! Gloucester is at your backs!
    Throw your slack bridles o'er the flurried manes,   10
    Ply well the rowel with faint trembling heels,
    Scampering to death at last!
FIRST KNIGHT: The enemy
    Bears his flaunt standard close upon their rear.
SECOND KNIGHT: Sure of a bloody prey, seeing the fens
    Will swamp them girth-deep.

STEPHEN: Over head and ears,
    No matter! 'Tis a gallant enemy;
    How like a comet he goes streaming on.
    But we must plague him in the flank,—hey, friends?
    We are well breath'd,—follow!

Enter EARL BALDWIN *and* SOLDIERS, *as defeated*

STEPHEN: De Redvers!
    What is the monstrous bugbear that can fright   20
    Baldwin?
BALDWIN: No scare-crow, but the fortunate star
    Of boisterous Chester, whose fell truncheon now
    Points level to the goal of victory.
    This way he comes, and if you would maintain
    Your person unaffronted by vile odds,
    Take horse, my Lord.
STEPHEN: And which way spur for life?
    Now I thank Heaven I am in the toils,
    That soldiers may bear witness how my arm
    Can burst the meshes. Not the eagle more
    Loves to beat up against a tyrannous blast,   30
    Than I to meet the torrent of my foes.
    This is a brag,—be't so,—but if I fall,
    Carve it upon my 'scutcheon'd sepulchre.
    On, fellow soldiers! Earl of Redvers, back!
    Not twenty Earls of Chester shall brow-beat
    The diadem.

                                                (Exeunt. Alarum

SCENE II. Another part of the Field

Trumpets sounding a Victory. Enter GLOCESTER, KNIGHTS, *and* FORCES

GLOCESTER: Now may we lift our bruised visors up,
    And take the flattering freshness of the air,

While the wide din of battle dies away
Into times past, yet to be echoed sure
In the silent ages of our chroniclers.

FIRST KNIGHT: Will Stephen's death be mark'd there, my good Lord,
Or that we gave him lodging in yon towers?

GLOCESTER: Fain would I know the great usurper's fate.

Enter TWO CAPTAINS *severally*

FIRST CAPTAIN: My Lord!

SECOND CAPTAIN: Most noble Earl!

FIRST CAPTAIN: The King—

SECOND CAPTAIN: The Empress greets—

GLOCESTER: What of the King?

FIRST CAPTAIN: He sole and lone maintains   10
A hopeless bustle mid our swarming arms,
And with a nimble savageness attacks,
Escapes, makes fiercer onset, then anew
Eludes death, giving death to most that dare
Trespass within the circuit of his sword!
He must by this have fallen. Baldwin is taken;
And for the Duke of Bretagne, like a stag
He flies, for the Welsh beagles to hunt down.
God save the Empress!

GOOCESTER: Now our dreaded Queen:
What message from her Highness?

SECOND CAPTAIN: Royal Maud   20
From the throng'd towers of Lincoln hath look'd down,
Like Pallas from the walls of Ilion,
And seen her enemies havock'd at her feet.
She greets most noble Gloster from her heart,
Intreating him, his captains, and brave knights,
To grace a banquet. The high city gates
Are envious which shall see your triumph pass;
The streets are full of music.

Enter SECOND KNIGHT

GLOCESTER: Whence come you?

SECOND KNIGHT: From Stephen, my good Prince,—Stephen!
    Stephen!

GLOCESTER: Why do you make such echoing of his name?   30

SECOND KNIGHT: Because I think, my lord, he is no man,
  But a fierce demon, 'nointed safe from wounds,
  And misbaptized with a Christian name.

GLOCESTER: A mighty soldier!—Does he still hold out?

SECOND KNIGHT: He shames our victory. His valour still
  Keeps elbow-room amid our eager swords,
  And holds our bladed falchions all aloof—
  His gleaming battle-axe being slaughter-sick,
  Smote on the morion of a Flemish knight,
  Broke short in his hand; upon the which he flung   40
  The heft away with such a vengeful force,
  It paunch'd the Earl of Chester's horse, who then
  Spleen-hearted came in full career at him.

GLOCESTER: Did no one take him at a vantage then?

SECOND KNIGHT: Three then with tiger leap upon him flew,
  Whom, with his sword swift-drawn and nimbly held,
  He stung away again, and stood to breathe,
  Smiling. Anon upon him rush'd once more
  A throng of foes, and in this renew'd strife,
  My sword met his and snapp'd off at the hilts.

GLOCESTER: Come, lead me to this Mars—and let us move
  In silence, not insulting his sad doom
  With clamorous trumpets. To the Empress bear
  My salutation as befits the time.

                         (*Exeunt* GLOCESTER *and* FORCES)

SCENE III. The Field of Battle

Enter STEPHEN *unarmed*

STEPHEN: Another sword! And what if I could seize
  One from Bellona's gleaming armoury,

154

Or choose the fairest of her sheaved spears!
Where are my enemies? Here, close at hand,
Here comes the testy brood. O, for a sword!
I'm faint—a biting sword! A noble sword!
A hedge-stake—or a ponderous stone to hurl
With brawny vengeance, like the labourer Cain
Come on! Farewell my kingdom, and all hail
Thou superb, plum'd, and helmeted renown,   10
All hail—I would not truck this brilliant day
To rule in Pylos with a Nestor's beard—
Come on!

Enter DE KAIMS *and* KNIGHTS, *etc.*

DE KAIMS: Is't madness or a hunger after death
    That makes thee thus unarm'd throw taunts at us?
    Yield, Stephen, or my sword's point dip in
    The gloomy current of a traitor's heart.
STEPHEN: Do it, De Kaims, I will not budge an inch.
DE KAIMS: Yes, of thy madness thou shalt take the meed.
STEPHEN: Darest thou?
DE KAIMS: How dare, against a man disarm'd?   20
STEPHEN: What weapons has the lion but himself?
    Come not near me, De Kaims, for by the price
    Of all the glory I have won this day,
    Being a king, I will not yield alive
    To any but the second man of the realm,
    Robert of Glocester.
DE KAIMS: Thou shalt vail to me.
STEPHEN: Shall I, when I have sworn against it, sir?
    Thou thinkst it brave to take a breathing king,
    That, on a court-day bow'd to haughty Maud,
    The awed presence-chamber may be bold   30
    To whisper, there's the man who took alive
    Stephen—me—prisoner. Certes, De Kaims,
    The ambition is a noble one.

DE KAIMS: 'Tis true,
  And, Stephen, I must compass it.
STEPHEN: No, no,
  Do not tempt me to throttle you on the gorge,
  Or with my gauntlet crush your hollow breast,
  Just when your knighthood is grown ripe and full
  For lordship.
A SOLDIER: Is an honest yeoman's spear
  Of no use at a need? Take that.
STEPHEN: Ah, dastard!
DE KAIMS: What, you are vulnerable! my prisoner!   40
STEPHEN: No, not yet. I disclaim it, and demand
  Death as a sovereign right unto a king
  Who 'sdains to yield to any but his peer,
  If not in title, yet in noble deeds,
  The Earl of Glocester. Stab to the hilts, De Kaims,
  For I will never by mean hands be led
  From this so famous field. Do ye hear! Be quick!
                  (*Trumpets. Enter the* EARL OF CHESTER *and* KNIGHTS

To GEORGE AND GEORGIANA KEATS
Saturday [*18 September 1819*]
    . . . A circumsta[n]ce [which] occur[r]ed lately at Dilkes—I think
it very rich and dramatic and quite illustrative of the little quiet fun
that he will enjoy sometimes. First I must tell you their house is at
the corner of Great Smith Street, so that some of the windows look
into one Street, and the back windows into another round the
corner—Dilke had some old people to dinner, I know not who—
but there were two old ladies among them—Brown was there—
they had known him from a Child. Brown is very pleasant with old
women, and on that day, it seems, behaved himself so winningly
they [*for* that] they became hand and glove together and a little
complimentary. Brown was obliged to depart early. He bid them
good bye and pass'd into the passage—no sooner was his back turn'd

than the old women began lauding him. When Brown had reach'd the Street door and was just going, Dilke threw up the Window and call'd 'Brown! Brown! They say you look younger than ever you did!' Brown went on and had just turn'd the corner into the other street when Dilke appeared at the back window crying "Brown! Brown! By God, they say you're handsome!" You see what a many words it requires to give any identity to a thing I could have told you in half a minute. . . .

To Autumn

1

SEASON of mists and mellow fruitfulness,
    Close bosom-friend of the maturing sun;
Conspiring with him how to load and bless
    With fruit the vines that round the thatch-eves run;
To bend with apples the moss'd cottage-trees,
    And fill all fruit with ripeness to the core;
        To swell the gourd, and plump the hazel shells
With a sweet kernel; to set budding more,
    And still more, later flowers for the bees,
    Until they think warm days will never cease,   10
        For Summer has o'er-brimm'd their clammy cells.

2

Who hath not seen thee oft amid thy store?
    Sometimes whoever seeks abroad may find
Thee sitting careless on a granary floor,
    Thy hair soft-lifted by the winnowing wind;
Or on a half-reap'd furrow sound asleep,
    Drows'd with the fume of poppies, while thy hook

Spares the next swath and all its twined flowers:
And sometimes like a gleaner thou dost keep
    Steady thy laden head across a brook;   20
    Or by a cyder-press, with patient look,
      Thou watchest the last oozings hours by hours.

3

Where are the songs of Spring? Ay, where are they?
    Think not of them, thou hast thy music too,—
While barred clouds bloom the soft-dying day,
    And touch the stubble-plains with rosy hue;
Then in a wailful choir the small gnats mourn
    Among the river sallows, borne aloft
      Or sinking as the light wind lives or dies;
And full-grown lambs loud bleat from hilly bourn;
    Hedge-crickets sing; and now with treble soft
The red-breast whistles from a garden-croft;
    And gathering swallows twitter in the skies.

To JOHN HAMILTON REYNOLDS
Tuesday [*21 Sept. 1819*]
   . . . How beautiful the season is now—How fine the air. A temperate sharpness about it. Really, without joking, chaste weather—Dian skies—I never lik'd stubble fields so much as now—Aye better than the chilly green of the spring. Somehow a stubble plain looks warm—in the same way that some pictures look warm—This struck me so much in my sunday's walk that I composed upon it. I hope you are better employed than in gaping after weather. I have been at different times so happy as not to know what weather it was—No I will not copy a parcel of verses. I always somehow associate Chatterton with autumn. He is the purest writer in the English Language. He has no French idiom, or particles like Chaucer—'tis genuine English Idiom in English words. I have given up Hyperion—there were too many Miltonic inversions in it—Miltonic verse

can not be written but in an artful or rather artist's humour. I wish
to give myself up to other sensations. English ought to be kept up.
It may be interesting to you to pick out some lines from Hyperion
and put a mark × to the false beauty proceeding from art, and one ||
to the true voice of feeling. Upon my soul 'twas imagination I
cannot make the distinction—Every now & then there is a Miltonic
intonation—But I cannot make the division properly. . . .

The Fall of Hyperion

A Dream

CANTO I

FANATICS have their dreams, wherewith they weave
A paradise for a sect; the savage too
From forth the loftiest fashion of his sleep
Guesses at Heaven: pity these have not
Trac'd upon vellum or wild indian leaf
The shadows of melodious utterance.
But bare of laurel they live, dream and die;
For Poesy alone can tell her dreams,
With the fine spell of words alone can save
Imagination from the sable charm   10
And dumb enchantment. Who alive can say
'Thou art no Poet; mayst not tell thy dreams'?
Since every man whose soul is not a clod
Hath visions, and would speak, if he had lov'd
And been well nurtured in his mother tongue
Whether the dream now purposed to rehearse
Be Poet's or Fanatic's will be known
When this warm scribe my hand is in the grave.

Methought I stood where trees of every clime,
Palm, myrtle, oak, and sycamore, and beech,   20
With Plantane, and spice blossoms, made a screen;
In neighbourhood of fountains, by the noise
Soft-showering in mine ears; and, by the touch
Of scent, not far from roses. Turning round,
I saw an arbour with a drooping roof
Of trellis vines, and bells, and larger blooms,
Like floral censers swinging light in air;
Before its wreathed doorway, on a mound
Of moss, was spread a feast of summer fruits,
Which nearer seen, seem'd refuse of a meal   30
By Angel tasted, or our Mother Eve;
For empty shells were scattered on the grass,
And grape stalks but half bare, and remnants more,
Sweet smelling, whose pure kinds I could not know.
Still was more plenty than the fabled horn
Thrice emptied could pour forth, at banqueting
For Proserpine return'd to her own fields,
Where the white heifers low. And appetite
More yearning than on earth I ever felt
Growing within, I ate deliciously;   40
And, after not long, thirsted, for thereby
Stood a cool vessel of transparent juice,
Sipp'd by the wander'd bee, the which I took,
And, pledging all the Mortals of the world,
And all the dead whose names are in our lips,
Drank. That full draught is parent of my theme.
No Asian poppy, nor Elixir fine
Of the soon fading jealous Caliphat;
No poison gender'd in close monkish cell
To thin the scarlet conclave of old men,   50
Could so have rapt unwilling life away.
Amongst the fragrant husks and berries crush'd,
Upon the grass I struggled hard against

160

The domineering potion; but in vain:
The cloudy swoon came on, and down I sunk
Like a Silenus on an antique vase.
How long I slumber'd 'tis a chance to guess.
When sense of life return'd, I started up
As if with wings; but the fair trees were gone,
The mossy mound and arbour were no more;   60
I look'd around upon the carved sides
Of an old sanctuary with roof august,
Builded so high, it seem'd that filmed clouds
Might spread beneath, as o'er the stars of heaven;
So old the place was, I remembered none
The like upon the earth: what I had seen
Of grey Cathedrals, buttress'd walls, rent towers,
The superannuations of sunk realms,
Or Nature's Rocks toil'd hard in waves and winds,
Seem'd but the faulture of decrepit things   70
To that eternal domed monument.
Upon the marble at my feet there lay
Store of strange vessels, and large draperies,
Which needs had been of dyed asbestos wove,
Or in that place the moth could not corrupt,
So white the linen; so, in some, distinct
Ran imageries from a sombre loom.
All in a mingled heap confus'd there lay
Robes, golden tongs, censer, and chafing dish,
Girdles, and chains, and holy jewelries—   80
    Turning from these with awe, once more I rais'd
My eyes to fathom the space every way;
The embossed roof, the silent massy range
Of columns north and south, ending in mist
Of nothing; then to Eastward, where black gates
Were shut against the sunrise evermore.
Then to the west I look'd, and saw far off
An Image, huge of feature as a cloud,

At level of whose feet an altar slept,
To be approach'd on either side by steps,   90
And marble balustrade, and patient travail
To count with toil the innumerable degrees.
Towards the altar sober-pac'd I went,
Repressing haste, as too unholy there;
And, coming nearer, saw beside the shrine
One minist'ring; and there arose a flame.
When in mid-May the sickening East Wind
Shifts sudden to the South, the small warm rain
Melts out the frozen incense from all flowers,
And fills the air with so much pleasant health   100
That even the dying man forgets his shroud;
Even so that lofty sacrificial fire,
Sending forth maian incense, spread around
Forgetfulness of everything but bliss,
And clouded all the altar with soft smoke,
From whose white fragrant curtains thus I heard
Language pronounc'd. 'If thou canst not ascend
These steps, die on that marble where thou art.
Thy flesh, near cousin to the common dust,
Will parch for lack of nutriment—thy bones   110
Will wither in a few years, and vanish so
That not the quickest eye could find a grain
Of what thou now art on that pavement cold.
The sands of thy short life are spent this hour,
And no hand in the universe can turn
Thy hour glass, if these gummed leaves be burnt
Ere thou canst mount up these immortal steps.'
I heard, I look'd: two senses both at once
So fine, so subtle, felt the tyranny
Of that fierce threat, and the hard task proposed.   120
Prodigious seem'd the toil, the leaves were yet
Burning,—when suddenly a palsied chill
Struck from the paved level up to my limbs,

And was ascending quick to put cold grasp
Upon those streams that pulse beside the throat:
I shriek'd; and the sharp anguish of my shriek
Stung my own ears—I strove hard to escape
The numbness; strove to gain the lowest step.
Slow, heavy, deadly was my pace: the cold
Grew stifling, suffocating, at the heart;   130
And when I clasp'd my hands I felt them not.
One minute before death, my iced foot touch'd
The lowest stair; and as it touch'd, life seem'd
To pour in at the toes: I mounted up,
As once fair Angels on a ladder flew
From the green turf to heaven.—'Holy Power,'
Cried I, approaching near the horned shrine,
'What am I that should so be sav'd from death?
What am I that another death come not
To choak my utterance sacrilegious here?'   140
Then said the veiled shadow—'Thou hast felt
What 'tis to die and live again before
Thy fated hour. That thou hadst power to do so
Is thy own safety; thou hast dated on
Thy doom.' 'High Prophetess,' said I, 'purge off
Benign, if so it please thee, my mind's film—'
'None can usurp this height,' returned that shade,
'But those to whom the miseries of the world
Are misery, and will not let them rest.
All else who find a haven in the world,   150
Where they may thoughtless sleep away their days,
If by a chance into this fane they come,
Rot on the pavement where thou rotted'st half—'
'Are there not thousands in the world,' said I,
Encourag'd by the sooth voice of the shade,
'Who love their fellows even to the death;
Who feel the giant agony of the world;
And more, like slaves to poor humanity,
163

Labour for mortal good? I sure should see
Other men here: but I am here alone.'   160
'They whom thou spak'st of are no vision'ries,'
Rejoin'd that voice—'they are no dreamers weak,
They seek no wonder but the human face;
No music but a happy-noted voice—
They come not here, they have no thought to come—
And thou art here, for thou art less than they—
What benefit canst thou do, or all thy tribe,
To the great world? Thou art a dreaming thing;
A fever of thyself—think of the Earth;
What bliss even in hope is there for thee?   170
What haven? every creature hath its home;
Every sole man hath days of joy and pain,
Whether his labours be sublime or low—
The pain alone; the joy alone; distinct:
Only the dreamer venoms all his days,
Bearing more woe than all his sins deserve.
Therefore, that happiness be somewhat shar'd,
Such things as thou art are admitted oft
Into like gardens thou didst pass erewhile,
And suffer'd in these Temples; for that cause   180
Thou standest safe beneath this statue's knees.'
'That I am favored for unworthiness,
By such propitious parley medicin'd
In sickness not ignoble, I rejoice,
Aye, and could weep for love of such award.'
So answer'd I, continuing, 'If it please,
Majestic shadow, tell me: sure not all
Those melodies sung into the world's ear
Are useless: sure a poet is a sage;
A humanist, Physician to all men.   190
That I am none I feel, as Vultures feel
They are no birds when Eagles are abroad.
What am I then? Thou spakest of my tribe:

164

What tribe?—The tall shade veil'd in drooping white
Then spake, so much more earnest, that the breath
Mov'd the thin linen folds that drooping hung
About a golden censer from the hand
Pendent.—'Art thou not of the dreamer tribe?
The poet and the dreamer are distinct,
Diverse, sheer opposite, antipodes.   200
The one pours out a balm upon the world,
The other vexes it.' Then shouted I
Spite of myself, and with a Pythia's spleen,
'Apollo! faded, farflown Apollo!

Where is thy misty pestilence to creep
Into the dwellings, thro' the door crannies,
Of all mock lyrists, large self-worshipers,
And careless Hectorers in proud bad verse.
Tho' I breathe death with them it will be life
To see them sprawl before me into graves.   210
Majestic shadow, tell me where I am,
Whose altar this; for whom this incense curls:
What Image this, whose face I cannot see,
For the broad marble knees; and who thou art,
Of accent feminine, so courteous.'
Then the tall shade, in drooping linens veil'd,
Spake out, so much more earnest, that her breath
Stirr'd the thin folds of gauze that drooping hung
About a golden censer from her hand
Pendent; and by her voice I knew she shed   220
Long-treasured tears. 'This temple sad and lone
Is all spar'd from the thunder of a war
Foughten long since by Giant Hierarchy
Against rebellion: this old Image here,
Whose carved features wrinkled as he fell,
Is Saturn's; I, Moneta, left supreme
Sole priestess of his desolation.'—

I had no words to answer; for my tongue,
Useless, could find about its roofed home
No syllable of a fit majesty   230
To make rejoinder to Moneta's mourn.
There was a silence while the altar's blaze
Was fainting for sweet food: I look'd thereon,
And on the paved floor, where nigh were pil'd
Faggots of cinnamon, and many heaps
Of other crisped spicewood—then again
I look'd upon the altar and its horns
Whiten'd with ashes, and its lang'rous flame,
And then upon the offerings again;
And so by turns—till sad Moneta cried,   240
'The sacrifice is done, but not the less,
Will I be kind to thee for thy goodwill.
My power, which to me is still a curse,
Shall be to thee a wonder; for the scenes
Still swooning vivid through my globed brain
With an electral changing misery
Thou shalt with those dull mortal eyes behold,
Free from all pain, if wonder pain thee not.'
As near as an immortal's sphered words
Could to a mother's soften, were these last: 250
But yet I had a terror of her robes,
And chiefly of the veils, that from her brow
Hung pale, and curtain'd her in mysteries
That made my heart too small to hold its blood.
This saw that Goddess, and with sacred hand
Parted the veils, Then saw I a wan face,
Not pin'd by human sorrows, but bright blanch'd
By an immortal sickness which kills not;
It works a constant change, which happy death
Can put no end to; deathwards progressing   260
To no death was that visage; it had pass'd
The lily and the snow; and beyond these

I must not think now, though I saw that face—
But for her eyes I should have fled away.
They held me back, with a benignant light,
Soft-mitigated by divinest lids
Half closed, and visionless entire they seem'd
Of all external things—they saw me not,
But in blank splendor beam'd like the mild moon,
Who comforts those she sees not, who knows not   270
What eyes are upward cast. As I had found
A grain of gold upon a mountain's side,
And twing'd with avarice strain'd out my eyes
To search its sullen entrails rich with ore,
So at the view of sad Moneta's brow,
I ached to see what things the hollow brain
Behind enwombed: what high tragedy
In the dark secret Chambers of her skull
Was acting, that could give so dread a stress
To her cold lips, and fill with such a light   280
Her planetary eyes; and touch her voice
With such a sorrow—'Shade of Memory!'
Cried I, with act adorant at her feet,
'By all the gloom hung round thy fallen house,
By this last Temple, by the golden age,
By great Apollo, thy dear foster child,
And by thyself, forlorn divinity,
The pale Omega of a wither'd race,
Let me behold, according as thou said'st,
What in thy brain so ferments to and fro.'—   290
No sooner had this conjuration pass'd
My devout lips; than side by side we stood,
(Like a stout bramble by a solemn Pine)
Deep in the shady sadness of a vale,
Far sunken from the healthy breath of morn,
Far from the fiery noon and Eve's one star.
Onward I look'd beneath the gloomy boughs,

And saw, what first I thought an Image huge,
Like to the image pedestal'd so high
In Saturn's Temple. Then Moneta's voice   300
Came brief upon mine ear,—'So Saturn sat
When he had lost his realms'—Whereon there grew
A power within me of enormous ken,
To see as a God sees, and take the depth
Of things as nimbly as the outward eye
Can size and shape pervade. The lofty theme
At those few words hung vast before my mind,
With half unravel'd web. I set myself
Upon an Eagle's watch, that I might see,
And seeing ne'er forget. No stir of life   310
Was in this shrouded vale, not so much air
As in the zoning of a summer's day
Robs not one light seed from the feather'd grass,
But where the dead leaf fell there did it rest.
A stream went voiceless by, still deaden'd more
By reason of the fallen Divinity
Spreading more shade: the Naiad 'mid her reeds
Press'd her cold finger closer to her lips.
Along the margin sand large footmarks went
No farther than to where old Saturn's feet   320
Had rested, and there slept, how long a sleep!
Degraded, cold, upon the sodden ground
His old right hand lay nerveless, listless dead,
Unsceptred; and his realmless eyes were clos'd,
While his bow'd head seem'd listening to the Earth,
His antient mother, for some comfort yet.

The Cap and Bells

XXIV

IT was the time when wholesale houses close
Their shutters with a moody sense of wealth,
But retail dealers, diligent, let loose
The gas (objected to on score of health),
Convey'd in little solder'd pipes by stealth,
And make it flare in many a brilliant form,
That all the powers of darkness it repell'th,
Which to the oil-trade doth great scaith and harm,
And supersedeth quite the use of the glow-worm.

XXV

Eban, untempted by the pastry-cooks,
(Of pastry he got store within the palace),
With hasty steps, wrapp'd cloak, and solemn looks,
Incognito upon his errand sallies,
His smelling-bottle ready for the allies;
He pass'd the hurdy-gurdies with disdain,
Vowing he'd have them sent aboard the gallies;
Just as he made his vow, it 'gan to rain,
Therefore he call'd a coach, and bade it drive amain.

XXVI

'I'll pull the string,' said he, and further said,
'Polluted jarvey! Ah, thou filthy hack!
Whose springs of life are all dried up and dead,
Whose linsey-wolsey lining hangs all slack,
Whose rug is straw, whose wholeness is a crack;

And evermore thy steps go clatter-clitter;
Whose glass once up can never be got back,
Who prov'st, with jolting arguments and bitter
That 'tis of modern use to travel in a litter.

XXVII

'Thou inconvenience! thou hungry crop
For all corn! thou snail-creeper to and fro,
Who while thou goest ever seem'st to stop,
And fiddle-faddle standest while you go;
I' the morning, freighted with a weight of woe,
Unto some lazar-house thou journeyest,
And in the evening tak'st a double row
Of dowdies, for some dance or party drest,
Besides the goods meanwhile thou movest east and west.

XXVIII

'By thy ungallant bearing and sad mien
An inch appears the utmost thou couldst budge;
Yet at the slightest nod, or hint, or sign,
Round to the curb-stone patient dost thou trudge,
School'd in a beckon, learned in a nudge,
A dull-eyed Argus watching for a fare;
Quiet and plodding thou dost bear no grudge
To whisking tilburies, or phaetons rare,
Curricles, or mail-coaches, swift beyond compare.'

To FANNY KEATS
Tuesday [*8 February 1820*]

Wentworth Place
Tuesday morn.

My dear Fanny—
    I had a slight return of fever last night, which terminated favour-
ably, and I am now tolerably well, though weak from small quantity

of food to which I am obliged to confine myself: I am sure a mouse would starv[e] upon it. Mrs Wylie came yesterday. I have a very pleasant room for a sick person. A Sopha bed is made up for me in the front Parlour which looks on to the grass plot as you remember Mrs Dilkes does. How much more comfortable than a dull room up stairs, where one gets tired of the pattern of the bed curtains. Besides I see all that passes—for instanc[e] now, this morning, if I had been in my own room I should not have seen the coals brought in. On sunday between the hours of twelve and one I descried a Pot boy. I conjectured it might be the one o'Clock beer—Old women with bobbins and red cloaks and unpresuming bonnets I see creeping about the heath. Gipseys after hare skins and silver spoons. Then goes by a fellow with a wooden clock under his arm that strikes a hundred and more. Then comes the old french emigrant, (who has been very well to do in france) whith his hands joined behind on his hips, and his face full of political schemes. Then passes Mr David Lewis a very goodnatured, goodlooking old gentleman whas [for who] has been very kind to Tom and George and me. As for those fellows the Brickmakers they are always passing to and fro. I mus'n't forget the two old maiden Ladies in well walk who have a Lap dog between them, that they are very anxious about. It is a corpulent Little Beast whom it is necessary to coax along with an ivory-tipp'd cane. Carlo our Neighbour Mrs Brawne's dog and it meet sometimes. Lappy thinks Carlo a devil of a fellow and so do his Mistresses. Well they may—he would sweep 'em all down at a run; all for the Joke of it. I shall desire him to pursue the fable of the Boys and the frogs: though he prefers the tongues and the Bones. You shall hear from me again the day after tomorrow—

Your affectionate Brother
John Keats

Wednesday Morng.

My dearest Girl,

I have been a walk this morning with a book in my hand, but as usual I have been occupied with nothing but you: I wish I could say in an agreeable manner. I am tormented day and night. They talk of my going to Italy. 'Tis certain I shall never recover if I am to be so long separate from you; yet with all this devotion to you I cannot persuade myself into any confidence of you. Past experience connected with the fact of my long separation from you gives me agonies which are scarcely to be talked of. When your mother comes I shall be very sudden and expert in asking her whether you have been to Mrs Dilke's, for she might say no to make me easy. I am literally worn to death, which seems my only recourse. I cannot forget what has pass'd. What? nothing with a man of the world, but to me deathful. I will get rid of this as much as possible. When you were in the habit of flirting with Brown you would have left off, could your own heart have felt one half of one pang mine did. Brown is a good sort of Man—he did not know he was doing me to death by inches. I feel the effect of every one of those hours in my side now; and for that cause, though he has done me many services, though I know his love and friendship for me, though at this moment I should be without pence were it not for his assistance, I will never see or speak to him until we are both old men, if we are to be. I *will* resent my heart having been made a football. You will call this madness. I have heard you say that it was not unpleasant to wait a few years—you have amusements— your mind is away—you have not brooded over one idea as I have, and how should you? You are to me an object intensely desireable— the air I breathe in a room empty of you is unhealthy. I am not the same to you—no—you can wait—you have a thousand activities— you can be happy without me. Any party, any thing to fill up the day has been enough. How have you pass'd this month? Who have you smil'd with? All this may seem savage in me. You do not feel as I do—you do not know what it is to love—one day you may—your time is not come. Ask yourself how many unhappy hours Keats has caused you in Loneliness. For myself I have been a Martyr the whole time, and for this reason I speak; the confession is forc'd from me by the torture. I appeal to you by the blood of that Christ you believe in: Do not write to me if you have done anything this month which it would have pained me to have seen. You may have altered—if you have not—if you still behave in dancing rooms and other societies as I have seen you—I do not want to live—if you have done so I wish this coming night may be my last. I cannot live without, and not only you but *chaste you; virtuous you*. The Sun rises and sets, the day passes, and you follow the bent of your inclination to a certain extent—you have no conception of the quantity of miserable feeling that passes through me in a day.—Be serious! Love is not a plaything—and again do not write unless you can do it with a crystal conscience. I would sooner die for want of you than——

Yours for ever

J. Keats

To CHARLES BROWN
Thursday 30 Nov. 1820

Rome. 30 November 1820.

My dear Brown,

'Tis the most difficult thing in the world to me to write a letter. My stomach continues so bad, that I feel it worse on opening any book,—yet I am much better than I was in Quarantine. Then I am afraid to encounter the proing and conning of any thing interesting to me in England. I have an habitual feeling of my real life having past, and that I am leading a posthumous existence. God knows how it would have been—but it appears to me—however, I will not speak of that subject. I must have been at Bedhampton nearly at the time you were writing to me from Chichester—how unfortunate—and to pass on the river too! There was my star predominant! I cannot answer any thing in your letter, which followed me from Naples to Rome, because I am afraid to look it over again. I am so weak (in mind) that I cannot bear the sight of any hand writing of a friend I love so much as I do you. Yet I ride the little horse,—and, at my worst, even in Quarantine, summoned up more puns, in a sort of desperation, in one week than in any year of my life. There is one thought enough to kill me—I have been well, healthy, alert &c, walking with her—and now—the knowledge of contrast, feeling for light and shade, all that information (primitive sense) necessary for a poem are great enemies to the recovery of the stomach. There, you rogue, I put you to the torture,—but you must bring your philosophy to bear—as I do mine, really—or how should I be able to live? Dr. Clarke is very attentive to me; he says, there is very little the matter with my lungs, but my stomach, he says, is very bad. I am well disappointed in hearing good news from George,—for it runs in my head we shall all die young. I have not written to ***** yet, which he must think very neglectful; being anxious to send him a good account of my health, I have delayed it from week to week. If I recover, I will do all in my power to correct the mistakes made during sickness; and if I should not, all my faults will be forgiven. I shall write to *** to-morrow, or next day. I will write to ***** in the middle of next week. Severn is very well, though he leads so dull a life with me. Remember me to all friends, and tell **** I should not have left London without taking leave of him, but from being so low in body and mind. Write to George as soon as you receive this, and tell him how I am, as far as you can guess;—and also a note to my sister—who walks about my imagination like a ghost—she is so like Tom. I can scarcely bid you good bye even in a letter. I always made an awkward bow.

God bless you!
John Keats

COMMENTARY

23. *Extract from* I STOOD TIP-TOE UPON A LITTLE HILL
This poem, which Keats left untitled in his *Poems* (1817), contains the story of Endymion, and for some time Keats spoke of it by that name. It was begun in the summer of 1816 on Hampstead Heath, but this passage is a reminiscence of a brook in the fields between Edmonton and Enfield. When a surgeon's apprentice at the former place, Keats used to pass this way to visit Charles Cowden Clarke at his old school, and he alludes to the same scene in his verse-epistle *To Charles Cowden Clarke*. This type of scenery is the background to many of Keats's poems.

24. *To* CHARLES COWDEN CLARKE, 9 Oct. [1816]
Author of the Sonnet to the Sun: possibly Horace Smith (1779–1849), poet, wit and contributor to Leigh Hunt's *The Examiner*; more likely Clarke himself.
Darwin: Erasmus Darwin (1731–1802), physician and minor poet.
those to G. Mathew: Keats refers to his *Epistle to George Felton Mathew*, another minor poet of his own age.
a Meeting: a Baptist chapel.

25. ON FIRST LOOKING INTO CHAPMAN'S HOMER
In October 1816 Keats read selected passages from a folio edition of the translation by George Chapman (1559?–1634) of Homer's *Iliad* and *Odyssey* with his friend Charles Cowden Clarke, and composed the sonnet early the next morning. The imagery of the poem follows the passages they read, which were from *Iliad*, Books 3, 5, and 13, and *Odyssey*, Book 5.
l.10. a new planet: probably alluding to the discovery of the planet Uranus by William Herschel on 13 March 1781, of which Keats had read in Bonnycastle's *Introduction to Astronomy*.
l.11. stout Cortez: the Pacific was discovered by Balboa in 1513. Keats was probably confusing two passages in *The History of America* by William Robertson.

25. KEEN, FITFUL GUSTS
Written after meeting Leigh Hunt in the middle of October 1816, and referring to his visits to Hunt's cottage in the Vale of Health, Hampstead, where they read or discussed, among other things, Milton's *Lycidas* and

Petrarch's sonnets to Laura. The influence of Hunt is seen in the weak rhymes in -y.

26. TO MY BROTHERS

Written on the birthday of his younger brother Thomas Keats (1799–1818) on 18 November 1816, and describing the lodgings he then shared with his two brothers at 76 Cheapside. The sonnet closely resembles Wordsworth's 'Personal Talk' sonnets (*Poems*, 1815).

26. TO HAYDON

Composed on 19 or 20 November 1816, and addressed to the historical painter Benjamin Robert Haydon, whom he had met at Hunt's in the previous month. In this sonnet, the influence of Wordsworth asserts itself strongly over that of Hunt, though both are associated with Haydon as 'Great spirits'; Keats probably had in mind Wordsworth's own sonnet beginning 'Great men have been among us'.

l.2 He of the cloud: Wordsworth, who lived within sight of Helvellyn.

l.5. He of the rose: Hunt, who when imprisoned for a libel on the Prince Regent from 1813 to 1815 converted his room in Horsemonger Lane Gaol into a bower with rose-trellised wallpaper.

l.13 Of mighty workings: the line was originally completed 'in a distant Mart'. Haydon himself suggested the omission of these words.

27. ON THE GRASSHOPPER AND THE CRICKET

Written on 30 December 1816, in competition with Leigh Hunt. It was common habit in Hunt's circle to write sonnets on a set subject in a set time, usually fifteen minutes. If these conditions were kept, Keats's sonnet is all the more remarkable. It only weakens at the end of the octave, where 'fun' and 'weed' show his difficulty in finding fourth rhymes in the pattern he had started, but it recovers triumphantly in the sestet.

28. *To* JOHN HAMILTON REYNOLDS, 17 April [1817]

quick freshes: The Tempest, III, ii, 77.

Birds eyes abate: The Bird's Eye flower (Germander Speedwell) closes in cold wet weather.

of all Loves: A Midsummer Night's Dream, II, ii, 154.

29. ON THE SEA

Written 17 April 1817 in the Isle of Wight in a letter to Reynolds (p. 28).

l.4. Hecate: goddess of the moon, thus controlling the tides.

30. *Extracts from* ENDYMION

Written from April to November 1817, revised early in 1818, and published in April of that year. In the autumn it was severely attacked by *Blackwood's*

Edinburgh Magazine and the *Quarterly Review*, but their criticism did not affect Keats as a poet. The passages given here are three of his own favourite sections of the poem, which is based on the Greek legend of Endymion, the shepherd king, loved by the moon goddess, Cynthia. The allegory of a young man's quest for love, which Keats makes of this, is vague and confused, and the verse uneven; but he often rises to heights of great lyric beauty and a deeper philosophy which foreshadows his later work.

BOOK I, *ll.*232–306. Generally known as the *Hymn to Pan*, this is a lyric interlude, spoken by a priest who is making sacrifice on behalf of the shepherds to Pan, the rural god.

l.236. hamadryad: a tree nymph.

l.243. Syrinx: Pan pursued a nymph named Syrinx, who changed into a reed to escape him.

l.247. turtles: turtle doves, as in Shakespeare's *The Phoenix and the Turtle.*

l.295. bourne: boundary, limit. Both the pantheistic philosophy and the expression of this passage owe much to Wordsworth; when Keats read it to him, the older poet called it 'a pretty piece of paganism'.

BOOK I, *ll.*777–842. When Keats revised the opening of this passage in January 1818, he told his publisher that the writing of these lines

> will perhaps be the greatest Service to me of any thing I ever did—It set before me at once the gradations of Happiness even like a kind of Pleasure Thermometer—and is my first Step towards the chief Attempt in the Drama—the playing of different Natures with Joy and Sorrow.

Keats's thought in this passage is that however far we are led by communion with the history and thought of all ages into spiritual heights, 'a fellowship with essence', human nature reaches its peak through love. While writing, in May 1817, he was reading Shakespeare's *Antony and Cleopatra*, from which he partly borrowed this philosophy and some of its expression.

*ll.*816–32. These lines and their expression are particularly reminiscent of *Antony and Cleopatra.*

*ll.*828–31. See *Romeo and Juliet*, III, v, 1–10.

34. *To* FANNY KEATS, 10 September 1817.
A Young Man: Benjamin Bailey of Magdalen Hall, Oxford.

35. LINES RHYMED IN A LETTER RECEIVED (BY J. H. R.) FROM OXFORD

Written in September 1817 to John Hamilton Reynolds, while Keats was staying in Oxford with Benjamin Bailey and composing the Third Book of *Endymion*. The lines are a parody of Wordsworth's minor poems 'in the

Style of School exercises'; they are also an amusing picture of Keats's stay in Oxford overlooking the deer-park of Magdalen College.

36. *To* BENJAMIN BAILEY, 22 Nov. 1817
certain ethereal Chemicals: the chemical liquid, ether, will extract substances from the inert mass over which it is poured.
this unpleasant affair: a letter from B. R. Haydon about Cripps, a young painter.
Adam's dream: Paradise Lost, VIII, 452–90.

38. *Extract from* ENDYMION
BOOK IV, *ll.*512–48. Keats here describes the mental state he sometimes expresses in his own letters; but he takes from it a philosophy, which he was later to develop in his famous 'Vale of Soul-making' letter, of the benefit to be derived from these dark states of the mind.
*l.*531.   *The death-watch tick:* the sound of the death-watch beetle.
*l.*536.   *Semele:* Semele was consumed by fire when pregnant with Bacchus, but the child was saved.
*l.*545.   *Carian:* Endymion, who according to some forms of the legend was a native of Caria in Asia Minor.

39. STANZAS
Written in December 1817, and perhaps associated with the Cave of Quietude passage in Book IV of *Endymion*.
*l.*21.   *The feel of not to feel it:* Keats's manuscripts have this expressive phrase. Printed versions substitute 'To know the change and feel it.'

40. *To* GEORGE AND THOMAS KEATS [21 Dec. 1817]
Penetralium: cited by Andrew Lang to prove that Keats 'had no classical education'.

41. ON MRS. REYNOLDS'S CAT
Written on 16 January 1818. A parody of Milton's sonnets, particularly those addressed to the Parliamentarian leaders, and beginning *Fairfax, Cromwell,* and *Vane.* Keats has several amusing passages about cats in his letters.

42. ON SITTING DOWN TO READ KING LEAR ONCE AGAIN
Written on 22 January 1818. Keats was revising his 'Romance' of *Endymion*, and planning the sterner epic of *Hyperion.* Much of his feeling about the contrast between his own two works is expressed in this sonnet. When he came to begin *Hyperion* later in the year, its opening was heavily based on *King Lear*, which he again re-read.

178

l.11.   the old oak Forest: the arduous pains of Shakespeare while writing *King Lear,* which Keats anticipates he himself will experience while writing *Hyperion.*

42.   *To* GEORGE AND THOMAS KEATS, 23 January 1818
A private theatrical: an amateur performance, where the audience were admitted free, and the performers paid for playing.
John Bull The Review . . . Bombastes Furioso: three early nineteenth-century plays.

43.   WHEN I HAVE FEARS
   Written towards the end of January 1818, this is Keats's first sonnet in the Shakespearian form. Though regarded as a prophecy of his early death, the thought is a commonplace with him.
l.3.   charact'ry: handwriting.
l.9   fair creature of an hour: Keats alludes to a chance meeting with an unknown lady in Vauxhall Gardens some years before. On 4 February 1818 he wrote another sonnet to her memory.

44.   LINES ON THE MERMAID TAVERN
   Supposed to have been written by Keats in February 1818 at the Mermaid Tavern itself, the haunt of Shakespeare, Ben Jonson and the Elizabethan poets. Here he treats the immortality of poets humorously; later in the year he returned to the subject more seriously in the poem 'Bards of Passion and of Mirth', written in the same form, which he called 'a sort of rondeau', i.e. in which the last lines echo the opening.

45.   *To* JOHN HAMILTON REYNOLDS, 19 Feb. 1818
the two-and-thirty Palaces: the thirty-two 'places of delight' of Buddhist doctrine.
an odd angle of the Isle: The Tempest, I, ii, 223.
puts a girdle round the earth: A Midsummer Night's Dream, II, i, 175.

47.   *Extract from* ISABELLA; OR THE POT OF BASIL
   Written mainly in March and April 1818 at Teignmouth, and perhaps revised later that year. Keats and J. H. Reynolds planned a joint volume of poetic versions of tales from Boccaccio's *Decameron.* The story of Isabella comes from *Decameron,* Fifth Story, Fourth Day. Keats wrote it in *ottava rima,* the Italian metre recently popularized by Byron, but he did not handle this as happily as the Spenserian stanzas of *The Eve of St. Agnes* or the couplets of *Lamia.* In fact, at one time he was unwilling to let *Isabella* appear in the

same volume as these other poems, and condemned the poem for 'inexperience', 'simplicity', and 'mawkishness'. He may have felt, with some reason, that in it he had reverted to the unfortunate style of Hunt's *Rimini*, and it is possible that the distractions of nursing his brother Tom, who was seriously ill at Teignmouth, took his mind off the poem. The section given here, in which Isabella's two brothers murder her lover Lorenzo, certainly flows more easily than much of the rest. Keats adds to Boccaccio's story the brothers' greedy ambition to marry Isabella to a rich suitor, and describes their economic position in a passage praised by Bernard Shaw for its realism.

*l.*107.   *swelt:* faint with heat.

*l.*109.   *Once proud-quiver'd:* once proud and now quivering.

*l.*124.   *lazar-stairs:* stairs where beggars sit.

*l.*135.   *Quick cat's-paws on the generous stray-away:* they pounced like cats on people of a careless and generous nature.

*l.*140.   *Hot Egypt's pest:* The Plagues of Egypt.

*l.*150.   *ghittern:* an instrument like a guitar.

*l.*158.   *gone:* dead, passed away.

*l.*159.   *stead:* serve.

*ll.*207–8.   A descent into the worst manner of Hunt's *Rimini*.

*l.*209.   *murder'd:* the dramatic effect of this anticipatory word was noted by Charles Lamb and others.

*l.*221.   *break-covert:* breaking from ambush.

51. *To* JOHN HAMILTON REYNOLDS, 3 May 1818
burden of the Mystery: Wordsworth, 'Tintern Abbey', *l.*38.

53. *To* THOMAS KEATS, Saturday 27 June 1818
mazy error over pendant shades: Paradise Lost, IV, 239.

54. OLD MEG
Written on 3 July 1818, between Dalbeattie and Auchencairn in the Lowlands of Scotland. Keats's companion, Charles Brown, described to him the character of Meg Merrilies from Walter Scott's *Guy Mannering*, which Keats had not read. After a picnic 'in Meg Merrilies county' Keats wrote the poem in a letter to his sister Fanny.

*l.*25.   *Margaret Queen:* Queen Margaret, wife of Henry VI, in one of Keats's favourite Shakespeare plays, *Richard III*.

*l.*28.   *a chip hat:* a hat made of wood fibre.

55. LINES WRITTEN IN THE HIGHLANDS AFTER VISIT TO BURNS'S
     COUNTRY
Written in the second half of July 1818. The poem has the metre and some of the thought of Wordsworth's *The Star-Gazers*.

l.22.   *Palmer's:* pilgrim's.
l.28.   *a Bard's low cradle-place:* the birthplace of Burns at Ayr, which Keats had just visited.

58. HYPERION: A FRAGMENT
    Written between autumn 1818 and spring 1819. The story of the poem opens when the second generation of gods, the Titans, has just been overthrown by a third, the Olympians. One of their number, Hyperion the Sungod, has not yet been dispossessed. The theme of the poem seems to have been his overthrow by Apollo, god of the sun, of healing and of poetry; it deals with the process of evolution from one form of life to another, and also with the making of a poet, symbolized by Apollo's assumption of his godhead from Mnemosyne, goddess of memory in Book III.
    One of Keats's reasons for giving up the poem at this point was that 'There were too many Miltonic inversions in it'. In point of fact, these only occur in certain passages, while much of the poem, particularly the opening, is strongly influenced by Dante's *Inferno* in Cary's translation and by Shakespeare's *King Lear* (for the picture of old Saturn) and *Troilus and Cressida* (for the debates of the Titans); its mythology is mainly derived from Ovid's *Metamorphoses* and other classical books Keats had read at school.

BOOK I, *ll*.1–19.   The interplay in these lines of the consonants *s* and *d* helps to give an impression of overwhelming sadness.
l.4.   *Saturn:* leader of the Titans, who had overthrown his own father Uranus or Coelus, and had now been overthrown by his own son, Jupiter.
l.30.   *Ixion's wheel:* to which he was bound in hell for punishment.
ll.52–72.   The address of Thea, Hyperion's wife, to Saturn resembles Cordelia's to the afflicted Lear, just as his own in *ll*.95–134 resembles Lear's speeches, though the style owes more to Milton and Spenser.
l.86.   *natural sculpture in cathedral cavern:* a clear memory of Keats's letter to Tom about Fingal's Cave (p. 57).
l.94.   *horrid:* bristling.
l.147.   *The rebel three:* Jupiter, Neptune and Pluto.
ll.158–212.   These lines, with their inversion and repetition, are the most consciously Miltonic in the whole poem. See Letter to Reynolds, p. 158.
l.274.   *colure:* one of two great circles dividing the heavens.

BOOK II, *ll*.1–38.   The imagery of the Titans' den again recalls Keats's letters to Tom (p. 53).
ll.19–20.   *Cœus . . . Porphyrion:* all gods and Titans, except Dolor, who was invented by Keats.

l.53.   *Caf:* another invention by Keats in this mythology, derived from the name of a mountain in the *Arabian Nights* and in Beckford's *Vathek*, which Keats read and which provides some of the atmosphere for the Titans' tortures.

l.78.   *Ops:* another name for Cybele, wife of Saturn. See Keats's letter to Woodhouse, 27 October 1818 (p. 88).

l.167.   *Athenian grove:* the Academy at Athens.

ll.172–244.   The speech of Oceanus contains much of what appears to be the theme of the poem. Keats always referred to *Hyperion* as an 'abstract' poem, and this abstract idea of universal evolution was probably in his mind.

ll.252–99.   The speech of Clymene continues that of Oceanus, and anticipates the fall of Hyperion to Apollo by the same process of evolution.

ll.373–75.   *Memnon:* son of Aurora, goddess of dawn. His statue was near Thebes in Egypt.

BOOK III, *ll*.3–7.   This invocation to the Muse probably marks a break in the poem caused by Tom Keats's death, to which it seems to refer.

ll.10–43.   The more lyrical style of this book is partly an attempt to express the poetic nature of Apollo, but partly due to a more lyric phase in Keats's life, after the strain of nursing Tom. The verse in this passage has several parallels with Chatterton's poem, *The Battle of Hastings*.

l.46.   *an awful Goddess:* Mnemosyne, goddess of Memory. She illustrates the Platonic idea that all knowledge is memory. By gazing on her, Apollo attains knowledge and immortality.

l.136.   Woodhouse, who transcribed the poem, completed the line in pencil
        Glory dawn'd: he was a god!

85.   *To* GEORGE AND GEORGIANA KEATS [14] Oct. 1818
particular: 'being particular' was 'making advances'. 'Charmian' (Miss Jane Cox) was too much at ease to think this unusual. See Smollett, *Humphry Clinker*.

86.   *To* GEORGE AND GEORGIANA KEATS [26] Oct. 1818
that same Lady: Mrs. Isabella Jones. Keats had first met her at Hastings at the end of May 1817, when he was writing *Endymion*.

87.   *To* RICHARD WOODHOUSE, 27 Oct. 1818
a thing per se and stands alone: Troilus and Cressida, I, ii, 15. *Saturn and Ops:* cf. *Hyperion*, II, 78–84.

89.   *To* GEORGE AND GEORGIANA KEATS [18 Dec.] 1818
wants: lacks.
not seventeen: Fanny Brawne was eighteen and a quarter, but appeared younger than her age.

89. ODE (BARDS OF PASSION AND OF MIRTH)
Written in December 1818. Although printed as an Ode, it is, as Keats said, 'a sort of rondeau' on the same theme as *Lines on the Mermaid Tavern* (see above).

91. FANCY
Another 'sort of rondeau,' written at the same time. Keats borrowed some of the thought from an essay by Leigh Hunt on the delights of sitting by the re in winter and imagining scenes of spring and summer.
.82. God of Torment: Pluto.

94. THE EVE OF ST. AGNES
Written late in January and early in February 1819, while on holiday at Chichester, Sussex, and Bedhampton, Hampshire. Some revisions made later in the year were disallowed by Keats's publishers. The Eve of St. Agnes is 20 January, and the subject of the poem was suggested to Keats by Isabella Jones at about that time. St. Agnes was a thirteen-year-old Christian martyr; her symbol was the lamb. According to legend, a girl who went supperless to bed on St. Agnes' Eve would have visions of her lover.
Keats had broken off the classical epic of *Hyperion*, and gone back to reading the Gothic 'Rowley' poems of Chatterton. The setting of his poem, however, is not literary, but highly visual, and derives from two visual experiences. Haydon the painter had just shown him prints of the fresco *The Triumph of Death* in the Camposanto at Pisa by an unknown fourteenth-century artist, and Keats was strongly moved by these. Secondly, he visited in Chichester a remarkable medieval building, containing the old Gildenhall of the City and the Hall of the Vicars' Choral, and at Stansted, Hampshire, an equally remarkable neo-Gothic Chapel. Physical details from all these sources colour the poem, and help to give it its rich and almost tangible setting. As a poem of young love beset with perils it has many obvious likenesses to Shakespeare's *Romeo and Juliet*, particularly stanzas x–xii.
l.5. Beadsman: a medieval retainer, to say prayers for the family. His 'beads' were the small stones or pieces of wood strung together to make a rosary.
l.16. orat'ries: oratories, places of prayer. See 'fireside orat'ries', *The Eve o, St. Mark, l.16.*
l.58. train: Keats's publishers misunderstood this word, until he put them right: 'I do not use *train* for *concourse of passers by* but for *Skirts* sweeping along the floor.'
l.70. amort: deadened. A coinage from his reading of Chatterton and Spenser. The whole poem is in the stanza-form of Spenser's *Faerie Queene*.

l.71.   St. Agnes and her lambs unshorn: on St. Agnes' Day, two lambs were blessed and shorn, and the wool woven by nuns into an archbishop's pall. See *ll.*105–07.

l.90.   beldame: old woman, derived from *The Minstrel* by James Beattie, a favourite poem of Keats's early days. She also recalls the Nurse in *Romeo and Juliet.*

l.120.   hold water in a witch's sieve: perform magic.

l.126.   mickle: plenty of.

l.172.   cates and dainties: delicious food. Keats added two elements to the legend, both derived from some French romances he was reading. One was that the hero should actually appear to the heroine; the other that he should prepare a feast, symbolizing their love.

l.174.   tambour-frame: drum-shaped embroidery frame.

l.217.   gules: heraldic name for red. The physical realism of this passage derives partly from the fact that Keats had seen at Stansted Chapel windows containing 'shielded scutcheons' predominately of this colour. The so-called anachronisms of the last two-thirds of the poem—stained glass in a bedroom, carpets, arras hangings—mark his use of the neo-Gothic setting at Stansted after the genuine medieval of Chichester.

l.266.   soother: more soothing. Another Chattertonian coinage.

l.292.   'La belle dame sans mercy': poem by Alain Chartier (1386–1458).

l.348.   mead: drink made from honey.

l.365.   an inmate owns: he recognizes Madeline, and does not bark. 'Inmate' meant an occupier of a dwelling.

l.377.   thousand aves: repetitions of the prayer, *Ave Maria.* Keats intended to revise these final lines thus:

> The beadsman stiffen'd, 'twixt a sigh and laugh
>
> Ta'en sudden from his beads by one weak little cough.

His intention was to make the poem more realistic, but his publishers objected.

107. THE EVE OF ST. MARK

Written 13–17 February 1819; the subject was probably suggested, like that of *The Eve of St. Agnes,* by Isabella Jones, whom Keats visited during that time. Whoever watches all night by the church door on St. Mark's Eve, 24 April, is supposed to see the ghosts of those who are to die the next year. The legend is given by Keats in the fake medieval language of the book which the heroine reads, but he never got beyond this point. The poem is like a series of medieval pictures; as such, it was highly valued by the Pre-Raphaelite painters of the mid-nineteenth century.

l.38.   golden mice: these were *inside* the Ark of the Covenant. I. Samuel. vi. 4. Bertha is reading a medieval illuminated manuscript, many of whose images

Keats took from the painted glass east window of Stansted Chapel, which he had visited on 25 January 1819.

l.79. Lima mice: lemur mice (see below).

l.81. Av'davat: correctly, amadavat, an Indian song-bird. The creatures embroidered on Bertha's firescreen all come from the East, with the exception of *Macaw*, an American parrot.

111. *To* GEORGE AND GEORGIANA KEATS, Friday 19 March 1819
'we all have one human heart': Wordsworth, 'The Old Cumberland Beggar,' *l.*152.

113. BRIGHT STAR (Final version)
Owing to a misunderstanding by Joseph Severn, whose recollections of matters concerning Keats were notably inaccurate, this poem was for a long time thought to be the last that Keats wrote; it appears as such in many collections. There is still a doubt when Keats wrote the first version; but the version printed here, which shows considerable revision in the sestet, was undoubtedly completed by the middle of April 1819. By that time, it had been copied by Fanny Brawne into Keats's copy of Dante's *Inferno*. Keats then wrote across it a cancelled opening for his sonnet *On a Dream* (see below). *Bright Star*, in this final version, therefore precedes *On a Dream*.

l.4. Eremite: hermit. The word is only used by Keats in a cancelled stanza of *The Eve of St. Agnes* and in *The Eve of St. Mark*, and may associate the sonnet with the time of those poems.

114. ON A DREAM
Written the middle of April 1819.

l.2. lulled Argus: 'As he had 100 eyes, of which only two were asleep at one time, Juno set him to watch Io, whom Jupiter had changed into a heifer: but Mercury, by order of Jupiter, slew him, by lulling all his eyes asleep with the sound of his lyre.' J. Lempriere, *A Classical Dictionary*, which Keats used at school.

l.10. the flaw: sudden gust. Cf. 'the flaw-blown sleet,' *The Eve of St. Agnes*, *l.*325.

l.11. lovers need not tell: Paolo and Francesca (the correct spellings) tell their sorrows to Dante in *Inferno*, V, 127–38.

115. LA BELLE DAME SANS MERCI
Written on 21 April 1819. A different version was printed in Leigh Hunt's *The Indicator* in 1820. This poem is closely connected with the sonnet *On a Dream* and the fifth canto of Dante's *Inferno*. Keats read this in the translation by H. F. Cary, and the short last line of each stanza is derived from Cary's way of breaking up his blank verse lines in translating this passage. The ballad

form is also connected with Keats's reading of Wordsworth, Robert Burton and Spenser's *Faerie Queene*; but the poem as a whole is one of the most spontaneous and unconscious of Keat's productions, scribbled late at night in a letter to his brother when he was very tired. There are signs that he himself did not think much of it, confirmed perhaps by the unfortunate alterations he allowed in the printed version. Its desolate atmosphere of fatal love echoes a theme common to many writers of the romantic movement.

l.39. La Belle Dame sans Merci: title of a lyric by Alain Chartier, a translation of which Keats read in his 1598 edition of Chaucer's works. See also *The Eve of St. Agnes, l.292.*

117. *To* GEORGE AND GEORGIANA KEATS [21 April 1819]
their Oromanes and their Vishnu: oriental deities. A short play entitled *Abudah; or, The Talisman of Oromanes* had just been presented at Drury Lane.

119. ODE TO PSYCHE
Written April 1819. Psyche, a mortal beauty, aroused the jealousy of Venus, who sent her son Cupid to torment her. He, however, fell in love with her, and visited her secretly by night, forbidding her to see his face; one night she lit a lamp, saw who her lover was, and was deserted by him; but after many trials they were reunited and married. The story is generally taken as an allegory of the soul (psyche), but Keats makes of her a goddess of beauty, who has not been properly worshipped; in the poem he imagines himself her priest, instituting the cult of beauty. The poem receives human colouring from the fact that in the month it was written Fanny Brawne, afterwards Keats's fiancée, came to live next door to him at Wentworth Place, which had a common garden with Keats's rooms. The style of the poem resembles Dryden's irregular odes, and has many likenesses to Milton, especially *Paradise Lost,* Book IV, the Garden of Eden.

l.2. By sweet enforcement: cf. Milton, *Lycidas, l.6.*
l.4. soft-conched: shaped like a shell but soft.
l.14. Tyrian: purple, from the purple dye of Tyre; but Keats wrote, and may have meant, 'Syrian.'
ll.32–35 and 46–49. Reminiscent of Milton, *Nativity Ode,* stanza xix.
l.41. lucent fans: shining wings.
l.60. With the wreathed trellis of a working brain: this striking image is partly derived from Keats's medical study of anatomy. Cf. 'branched thoughts,' *l.52* above.

121. ODE ON INDOLENCE
The thought and the imagery of this Ode, which was not published in Keats's lifetime, are obviously suggested by those of his letter of 19 March 1819 to George Keats (see p. 111). He probably re-read this part of the letter

when he finally sent it off, about 3 May 1819, and tried to reconstruct the experience, but in a setting of early May (see *l.26*). It is also noticeable that the expression 'my idle spright' (*l.59*) is repeated exactly from the sonnet *On a Dream* (p. 114), which he wrote in the middle of April.

The Ode, though written just after the *Ode to Psyche*, shows Keats still experimenting with the form he was to develop in the later Odes. It is repetitive and loose in construction, lacking their concentration and clarity. It is not even certain in what order he wrote the stanzas, and the scheme adopted here is that favoured by H. W. Garrod. It must be added that Keats himself wrote (9 June) 'You will judge of my 1819 temper when I tell you that the thing I have most enjoyed this year has been writing an ode to Indolence.'

l.10. *Phidian:* relating to Pheidias, the Greek sculptor. Keats means he knows about sculpture but not about vases.

ll.57–58. *visions for the night, And for the day:* a reminiscence of his reading for the *Ode to Psyche* in *The Golden Asse*, chap. xxi, 'as the visions of the day are accounted false and untrue, so the visions of the night do often chance contrary.'

123. *To* FANNY KEATS [1 May 1819]
one of Birkbeck's sons: Richard Birkbeck was going to join his father Morris Birkbeck, who had founded the English settlement in Illinois. George Keats did not in fact join Birkbeck's settlement, but set up in trade at Louisville, Kentucky.

a nice Clergyman: Fanny Keats was being prepared for Confirmation.

a cellar a mile deep . . . Flora: cf. *Ode to a Nightingale*, stanza II.

124. ODE TO A NIGHTINGALE
Written early in May 1819. According to Charles Brown, it was inspired by the song of an actual nightingale in the garden at Wentworth Place. The poem contrasts the realities of human life and death with the ideal world of natural beauty, typified by the nightingale's song, the same through all the passing generations of man; yet the conclusion hints that this too may be a fancy that has deceived the poet. Much of the scenery of the poem is reminiscent of Keats's favourite Chaucerian poem *The Flower and the Leaf*.

l.4. *Lethe-wards:* towards the river of forgetfulness, insensibility.

l.7. *Dryad:* wood-nymph. The poem originally opened 'small winged dryad'.

l.13. *Flora:* goddess of flowers. Keats wrote, on 1 May, 'say your prayers to Flora'. She leads the dance in *The Flower and the Leaf*.

l.14. *Provençal song:* the songs of the troubadours of Southern France.

l.16. *Hippocrene:* the spring on Mount Helicon, sacred to the Muses.

l.26. Keats himself said that this line referred to his brother Tom's death.

*l.*60. *requiem:* a funeral chant over the dead poet.

*l.*64. *clown:* peasant.

*ll.*66–67. *Ruth:* Keats has combined two episodes from the *Book of Ruth* with an unconscious memory of Wordsworth's poem, *The Solitary Reaper.*

*l.*68. The boldness of ending this line with a completely unstressed word gives the two famous lines that follow their strength and inevitability.

124. ODE ON A GRECIAN URN

Written May 1819. Just as the *Ode to a Nightingale* contrasts the world of natural beauty with the trials of human life, so this ode contrasts them with the world of art, typified in the unchanging figures on a Greek vase. Keats did not take the urn of the poem from any particular known vase, but from several shown in engravings by Henry Moses and by F. and P. Piranesi, mixed perhaps with images from the Elgin Marbles and from French classical paintings. The permanence of this ideal work of art is set against the fever and impermanence of human endeavour. Wordsworth had anticipated this idea in a sonnet, which Keats perhaps read.

*l.*7. *Tempe:* a vale in Thessaly.

*l.*7. *Arcady:* Arcadia, a district of Greece.

*ll.*11–12. *Heard melodies . . . sweeter:* even music is more permanent when one cannot hear the melodist who plays it, but when one receives a spiritual impression of it.

*l.*28. *breathing:* living.

*ll.*29–30. Compare *Ode to a Nightingale,* stanza III.

*l.*41. *O Attic shape! Fair attitude!:* not a clumsiness, but a deliberate use of sound in an almost Elizabethan way, in which Shakespeare would have delighted. Some critics have found weakness in this last stanza.

*l.*41. *brede:* embroidery, ornament.

*l.*45. *Cold Pastoral!:* cold, because carved in marble.

*ll.*49–50.   *Beauty is truth, truth beauty, that is all*
                Ye know on earth, and all ye need to know.

The message of the poem is contained in this message of the Urn to those who regard it. This Platonic identification of truth with beauty was always close to Keats's thought, and appears not only in his letters but in his conversation. Severn quotes him as saying of Greek art and the spirit of the past that 'It's an immortal youth, just as there is no *Now* or *Then* for the Holy Ghost.' In the stress of this time of his life, this view of the essential truth of imagination speaking through the beauty of art struck Keats most forcibly, and gave rise to the almost proverbial expression with which the poem ends.

129. ODE ON MELANCHOLY

Written May or June 1819. Keats was reading *The Anatomy of Melancholy* by Robert Burton, and he took the general idea of the poem from the section of this book, 'Against Melancholy it self', arguing that the man subject to melancholy should make the best use of his moods. He also seems to echo the statement earlier in Burton that the Romans worshipped the Goddess of Melancholy in the temple of the Goddess of Pleasure (*ll*.25–26). The thought, however, that trials and depressions are a necessary part of the progress of the soul is paramount in Keats at this time. This ode, which he revised in the autumn (perhaps then cancelling an original first stanza), helped to create the picture of the veiled priestess in *The Fall of Hyperion*. It also harks back to the Cave of Quietude passage in *Endymion*.

l.1. The abrupt opening is perhaps due to the cancellation of a previous stanza.

l.6. *beetle:* death-watch beetle, as in *Endymion*, IV, 531.

l.6. *death-moth:* correctly, death's head moth.

l.7. *Psyche:* loved one; here with some suggestion of companion *soul*.

ll.21–24. Compare *Ode to a Nightingale*, stanza III.

ll.26–27. This intensely physical image tends to confirm the stories of Keats's drinking habits, such as that told by the painter B. R. Haydon, who said that Keats 'covered his tongue & throat as far as he could reach with cayenne pepper' in order the enjoy the 'delicious coolness of claret'.

130. LAMIA

Written June/July 1819 (Part I) and in September (Part II), *Lamia* is the most consciously artistic of all Keats's productions, written 'with great care, after much studying of Dryden's versification.' Brown, who made this comment, had persuaded Keats in June 1819 to try and write a poem that would popular with the public as a way of solving his money difficulties. Keats found the story in Burton's *Anatomy of Melancholy*, and saw at once that it would give the public what he called 'a sensation.' He also wished to write in a far more realistic style, and get rid of the 'mawkishness' and 'inexperience of life,' which, he felt, marred *Isabella* and even *The Eve of St. Agnes*. The result was a poem which has often puzzled critics by what they have considered its cynical or cheap touches (cf. Part I, *ll*.328–32 and Part II, *ll*. 229–38), but which probably represents Keats's desire to make his poetry more in tune with 'men and women'.

The story tells how Hermes grants human shape to a serpent (Lamia), who, as a beautiful woman, captivates a young Corinthian philosopher, Lycius. They live in a magical palace, until he persuades her to have a wedding feast; to this, uninvited, comes his old tutor, Apollonius, who exposes her as a serpent, at which she vanishes and Lycius dies. The story is clearly capable of allegory, and Keats has been criticized for appearing to defend sexual love against 'philosophy' (see the passage from Part II mentioned above) and indulging in masochistic fantasy (Part II, *ll*.70–83); but these fall into place if one remembers his aim in this poem to show the whole of human life. Attempts to fit the allegory to his own situation—e.g. himself as Lycius, Fanny Brawne as Lamia, Charles Brown as Apollonius—are unconvincing, though he undoubtedly drew on a wide range of personal experience. The Drydenian metre, with many triplets and alexandrines, is handled with great sureness, and suits, as he intended, the sophisticated tone of the poem, which he printed first in his 1820 volume.

PART I:

l.7. *ever-smitten Hermes:* the messenger of the Gods, continually falling in love, as told in Ovid, *Metamorphoses.*

l.46. *cirque-couchant:* lying coiled in a circle.

l.47. *gordian:* intricate, like the knot tied by Gordius of Phrygia.

ll.47–58. This passage is based on a remarkable piece of prose in Burton's *Anatomy of Melancholy.*

l.58. *Ariadne's tiar:* crown given to Ariadne by Bacchus, afterwards made a constellation.

l.78. *Phœbean dart:* sunbeam.

l.81. *star of Lethe:* Hermes, who guided the dead beyond Lethe.

l.115. *Circean:* like Circe, the sorceress.

l.148. *besprent:* sprinkled.

l.155. *volcanian yellow:* sulphur.

l.174. *Cenchreas:* town on the Isthmus of Corinth.

l.191. *sciential:* endowed with knowledge. Lamia is described as being as scientific in love as Apollonius is in natural philosophy.

l.198. *unshent:* unspoilt.

l.211. *palatine:* of a palace. Keats uses the word in his letters.

l.212. *Mulciber:* Vulcan.

l.212. *piazzian:* like a colonnade. Keats probably coined this from the Piazza at Covent Garden.

l.236. *Platonic shades:* the philosophical ideas of Plato.

l.320. *The Adonian feast:* the feast of Adonis, when flowers were placed by his statue.

l.329. *Peris:* good angels. A Persian term; Lamia's servants are also Persian (Part I, *l.*390).

l.333. *Pyrrha's pebbles:* the pebbles cast after the Flood by Deucalion and Pyrrha grew as men and women.

l.347. *comprized:* wrapped up.

ll.350–61. A wonderfully realistic picture of a walk at night through a great city.

l.349. *flitter-winged:* able to flit in everywhere, like a bat.

l.16. For all this: despite all this.

l.39. passion's passing bell: the death of passion. The opposition between thought and passionate love is continued from this line throughout the rest of the poem.

l.80. The serpent: the Python, killed by Apollo.

l.80. certes: surely (archaic). Used by Keats in *Otho the Great* and *King Stephen*, derived from Cary's translation of Dante's *Inferno*, from which Keats drew his serpent imagery.

l.136. missioned: commissioned. See *The Eve of St. Agnes, l.193.*

l.160. daft: resisted.

l.285. libbard's: leopard's (archaic).

l.224. willow: the plant of grief, weeping.

l.226. thyrsus: Bacchus's staff, intoxication.

l.231. an awful rainbow: as early as 21 December 1817, Keats had written 'in these cold and enfeebling times . . . The goblin is driven from the hearth, and the rainbow is robbed of its mystery', and a week later he blamed Sir Isaac Newton and the natural philosophers for this. Attacks on 'philosophy' or science were a poetic commonplace (cf. Wordsworth, *A Poet's Epitaph*).

l.236. gnomed: home of goblins (see above).

l.277. juggling: with power to bewitch.

l.291. sophist: teacher of knowledge.

l.301. perceant: piercing.

151. KING STEPHEN: a fragment

Written August 1819, at Winchester, when Keats had just finished writing the tragedy of *Otho the Great* in collaboration with Charles Brown. Brown gives this account of the fragment:

> As soon as Keats had finished *Otho the great*, I pointed out to him a subject for an english historical tragedy in the reign of Stephen . . . He was struck with the variety of events and characters which must necessarily be introduced; and I offered to give, as before, their dramatic conduct. 'The play must open', I began, 'with the field of battle, when Stephen's forces are retreating—' 'Stop!' he said, 'stop! I have been already too long in leading-strings. I will do all this myself.' He immediately set about it, and wrote two or three scenes, about 130 lines.

The scenes resemble of one Keats's favourite plays, *Richard III*, and were clearly designed for the actor he so much admired, Edmund Kean. The play was given up on his hearing the (false) news that Kean was leaving the country that autumn. He seems to have added later a fourth scene of much less merit, but the three printed here show real dramatic ability, and prove that he might have achieved, in his own words, 'the writing of a few fine Plays—my greatest ambition'.

157. TO AUTUMN

Written 19 September 1819, at Winchester, after his favourite walk there, which he describes in his letters (see p. 158). Keats had worked through from the passionate questionings of the early summer odes to a mood of acceptance. Although there is no explicit statement of the philosophy of the ode, as there had been in the *Ode on a Grecian Urn*, it is implicit in the lines that since decay is inevitable, we should accept it as a part of life. Technically, the poem was a new achievement for Keats, composed, as he wished, without the 'fever' of his poetic output that summer. 'The poet himself is completely lost in his images, and the images are presented as meaning simply themselves: Keats's richest utterance is the barest of metaphor.' Aileen Ward, *John Keats: The Making of a Poet*, page 322. Keats at this time was impressed by what he considered the 'purity' of Chatterton's poems, and the poem in its first draft was even more like some passages from Chatterton's *Aella*, which contains a stanza to Autumn. It also echoes some of the moments of 'brief pathos' in Dante's *Inferno*.

ll.12–22. Autumn is personified going about the various tasks of the season.
l.18. *the next swath:* the next line of corn to be cut.
l.28. *sallows:* willows. Printed 'shallows', but Keats originally wrote 'sallows'. See 'I stood tip-toe', *l*.67.

159. THE FALL OF HYPERION

These 326 lines take us to the opening scene of the previous *Hyperion*, and seem to have been written at Winchester in September 1819. When Keats returned to London, he tried to continue welding the old poem on to the new for about another 200 lines. His decision at Winchester to give up *Hyperion* (p. 158) probably refers, however, to both versions, and his later work on it seems to have been desultory.

Although these lines in one sense form a new prologue to the poem, in another they take up where the former poem left off: it is now Keats who is initiated into Knowledge by Moneta, another name of Mnemosyne who initiated Apollo. The agony felt by Apollo is now felt by Keats personally in the most impressive part of this fragment. The subjective form of the new poem is derived from Dante's *Inferno*.

l.10. *sable charm:* in some versions, *chain*. *Charm* seems intended, since the sense of the passage seems to be that fanatics (religious men) and savages (primitive men) both have visions, but lack the poet's power to turn these imaginatively into poetry; with them they remain as a sable charm (religion)

or a dumb enchantment (superstition). Whether Keats's vision is that of true
poetry will be judged by posterity.

*ll.*19–56.   These lines are full of reminiscences of the Odes Keats had written
that summer.

*l.*35.   *fabled horn:* the cornucopia.

*l.*48.   *Caliphat:* the Caliphate, the government of the Moslem world.

*l.*50.   *scarlet conclave:* the assembly of Cardinals.

*ll.*61–71.   These lines, even more than those in *Hyperion*, echo Keats's letter
to Tom on Fingal's Cave. He had just rediscovered this letter and was copying
it for George.

*ll.*107–36.   These lines are both reminiscent of the trials of Dante in the
Inferno and of the growing symptoms of tuberculosis in Keats.

*ll.*187–210.   Keats seems to have intended to cancel these lines, which spring
from his temporary disillusion with himself as a poet. As they stand, they
contradict the opening of the poem, since the true and imaginative dream is
poetry. Moneta's argument has been that even the dreamer who is a true poet
is less worthy that those who simply do good; Keats here echoes his letter
to Reynolds a few weeks before, 'that fine writing is next to fine doing the
top thing in the world'.

169.   *Extract from* THE CAP AND BELLS
   Written during the winter of 1819–20. This last poem of Keats's life has
been unjustly neglected, partly because not generally understood. On the sur-
face it appears to be a rather pointless fairy-tale in verse; in fact, it is a satire
on some of the poets and literary groups of the time, in the manner of certain
passages in Byron's *Don Juan*, canto one, which had just appeared. It is set
in London, and has many contemporary touches; some of the best are in these
selected stanzas. Eban, the palace-servant, is identified by many personal
details as William Hazlitt, the essayist and polemical writer. His diatribe about
the hackney-coachman is precisely like Hazlitt's attacks on various literary
persons, which Keats quoted with approval in his letters. Keats's treatment of
the story grew weak and inconsistent as he himself grew ill, and he never
finished it; but it is one of the few poems that combines the humour and gusto
of the letters with real poetry.

XXIV, *l.*4.   *The gas:* London was not commonly lit by gas until 1816. Many
householders were still fearful of using it for domestic purposes.

170.   *To* FANNY KEATS, 8 February 1820
fever: Keats had been taken ill on Thursday 3 February. The fever and blood-
spitting of this attack clearly announced tuberculosis.

the tongues and the Bones: cf. *A Midsummer Night's Dream*, IV, i, 33: *Bottom,* 'let us have the tongs and the bones'. The pun is typical of Keats, even in his illness.

172. *To* FANNY BRAWNE [June] 1820

Generally dated July, but MacGillivray, *Keats*, p. xxxv, shows it belongs to June, before Keats's second and more severe set of haemorrhages. Keats had spent the month of May separated from Fanny and living near Leigh Hunt in Kentish Town. His growing illness led him to brood on some small incident (probably an unchaperoned visit to the Dilkes at Westminster (see p. 156)), and this jealous outburst was the result.

173. *To* CHARLES BROWN 30 Nov. 1820

to pass me on the river: Brown returned by boat from a holiday in Scotland, and, unknown to both, had anchored off Gravesend within hailing distance of the boat taking Keats to Italy.

walking with her: he refers to Fanny Brawne.

*****: The asterisks represent the names of various other friends deleted by Brown in copying the letter. One might guess that they were Haslam, Dilke, Woodhouse, and Reynolds respectively.

INDEX OF SOME TOPICS IN THE LETTERS

INDEX OF TITLES AND FIRST LINES OF POEMS